Domestic Violence and Family Safety
A systemic approach to working with violence in families

Domestic Violence and Family Safety

A systemic approach to
working with violence in families

by

JAN COOPER MSc
and **ARLENE VETERE** PhD

Reading Safer Families,
Reading, Berkshire

W
WHURR PUBLISHERS
LONDON AND PHILADELPHIA

© 2005 Whurr Publishers Ltd
First published 2005
by Whurr Publishers Ltd
19b Compton Terrace
London N1 2UN, England and
325 Chestnut Street, Philadelphia PA 19106, USA

Reprinted 2006

British Library Cataloguing in Publication Data

A catalogue record for this book
is available from the British Library.

ISBN-10: 1 86156 477 5 p/b
ISBN-13: 978 1 86156 477 1 p/b

Contents

Foreword

Jan Cooper and Arlene Vetere have published an important text on *Domestic Violence and Family Safety*, which introduces a systemic approach to working with violence in families. The main emphasis of work in the domestic violence field in the United Kingdom and elsewhere is to provide services for safety for women and children through the work of the Women's Aid Movement. In the area where the authors work in Reading in Berkshire, there are houses available for women to find safety. But what continues to be a problem is the nature of the response to men's violent behaviour. Providing therapeutic services for men as perpetrators is not a politically popular action, the majority of community responses having been properly protecting towards women and children. Interventions for men have principally been available through the criminal justice system which requires a conviction and there are very few therapeutic projects open to men in the community generally. There is now recognition that children who are exposed to domestic violence may be harmed, as if they were themselves being abused. Indeed there is a significantly higher risk that children will themselves be abused directly if they live in a context where domestic violence has been perpetrated. Yet the therapeutic resources are not available for those men perpetrating violent action.

The Reading Safer Families is a specialist community based project in the independent sector which has now been working for a period of eight years. They observe that most of the men they have worked with have been child witnesses to domestic violence, and have often been battered and abused themselves. It is essential that there is broad access to therapeutic resources for these individuals and that programmes of work need to include issues for them as fathers, and to understand their responsibilities as fathers as well as partners. A second area which needs attention is mothers and their children, especially sibling groups. An extensive review of the impact of domestic violence on children's development is provided. It is essential that services are available to help caring parents support children who have been traumatised through witnessing experiences of violence themselves, breaking the intergenerational pattern of violence as a response to stressful contexts.

The community is now gaining more understanding about domestic violence, responses are becoming more complex, there is an understanding that women can be violent as well as men. It is essential that practitioners whose orientation is towards the family as a locus for treatment and who are concerned about the extensive impact of violence on family life, should consider how they can work with this very considerable problem. Jan Cooper and Arlene Vetere in their approach to working with family violence in the Reading Safer Families Project provide an excellent model to help systemic practitioners undertake this approach and are also introducing an approach which would be of considerable value were it to be reproduced in other parts of the country. There has been considerable resistance to the idea of working with domestic violence with couples jointly, and the emphasis has been on separate working. Yet recent research which has been reviewed by Jan Cooper and Arlene Vetere illustrates that domestic violence – focussed therapy, with carefully screened couples, appears to be at least as effective in reducing abusive behaviour as men's groups and individual treatment for men. Experiences of working with upwards of 400 families and couples are described. In many there have been extensive contact with court assessments, child care proceedings or child custody contact disputes. A key approach to their work has been a constant focus on issues of risk, responsibility and collaboration. They devote a considerable time in their approach, working with individuals as well as the couples together, helping them develop safety in relationships.

They have adopted a key approach in their therapeutic work that is important in all therapeutic work in the field of violence, which is the need for a supportive agency who can ensure safety. This can be Social Services, a general practitioner, recognising that a therapeutic team focuses on testing the capacity for change, testing the ability of the family members to achieve a no violence contract, but that another agency needs to support the family and ensure safety during the process of work creating a sustainable network of safety.

They lay considerable emphasis on issues of responsibility, holding the tension essential in therapeutic work between the responsibilities which need to be taken for violent behaviour on the one hand, and explanations for violence on the other. They ensure that explanations are not used to minimise or to deny violent intent and action. This is a key element in therapeutic work which seeks both to understand, and to take an appropriate level of responsibility. Jan Cooper and Arlene Vetere point out from a moral relationships standpoint the ability to take responsibility for violent behaviour, and to be held accountable for what we do and the consequences for others and our relationships to be the highest context marker for therapeutic work. They point out that it is essential that there is a no-confidentiality approach to the work, an essential ingredient in breaking the code of secrecy which is such an essential element of violent behaviour. They achieve this goal by ensuring that there is close contact with individuals as well as the couple, and a rule of open communication – an unusual approach for families seeking therapy in the ordinary situation – essential when violence has occurred.

In their approach Jan Cooper and Arlene Vetere call on a wide variety of theories to help understand both the process of violence within families and between couples, and in assisting in the development of the work. The overall approaches have a systemic understanding and approach to intervention, but use different approaches to the detailed aspect of the work to create a coherent whole. They use multiple theories to understand the many layered situations which are met, they link the history of emotional relationships and family developments, and the dilemmas and binds within these relationships which intersect with violence, coercion and the abuse of power. They ensure that evidence based approaches are used where appropriate, and that there is a requirement for changes in behaviour, in beliefs, in emotional patterns and attachments and in relationships with social contexts developing a capacity to cooperate with professional workers and community members. They use a holistic multi-dimensional and multi-perspective approach. They use feminist informed thinking, social learning theories, and ensure that effective evidence based approaches to managing anger and arousal stemming from the cognitive behavioural traditions are used. They also pay very considerable attention to the appropriate use of language and to encourage the idea that changes in behaviour, beliefs and relationships are possible, and that women can reclaim a sense of 'independent subjectivity and agency', and men can 'accept responsibility for their behaviour and their dependency needs' and 'empathise with the experiences of those who have been harmed.'

They use an interesting approach to the work by having a lead therapist and a reflecting note-taking colleague in the room. This provides the opportunity for continuous observation and reflectivity which is a key aspect of the work in enabling family members to move from a context of action to thought. They feel that using this approach there can be clarity and openness, different perspectives can be harnessed, and there can be a co-evolution of therapeutic processes. Given the intensity of the emotional context with which they are working, having the opportunity of a shared approach and perspective is of considerable value.

Some helpful case studies are provided which give considerable insight into the process of work. The authors also demonstrate that it is possible not only to work as a therapist, but also to use therapeutic experiences to help provide an expert witness approach in the court's themselves, and a context for sharing and training others in the field. There is a great deal of value to practitioners and to policy makers in the approach described. There is a considerable gap in therapeutic services for family violence. There is now an Intergovernmental Initiative on tackling family violence at all levels. Jan Cooper and Arlene Vetere's contribution to this current debate will be of considerable value for those families who continue to suffer the devastating effects of family violence.

Dr Arnon Bentovim

Introduction

Eight years ago, we established Reading Safer Families as an independent community project dedicated to working with violence in family relationships (Vetere and Cooper, 2003). Reading Safer Families was part of the Safer Families Project, which included London and Oxford. Jan is a family therapist and former psychiatric social worker and Arlene a family therapist and clinical and academic psychologist. The combination of the different professional trainings, experiences in different agencies, both statutory and voluntary, and the commitment to systemic work has proved important in the quality and scope of the service offered. This book outlines our theoretical approach to assessment, rehabilitation and therapy when working with violence in family relationships and the associated ethical problems. We identify three recurrent themes: risk, responsibility and collaboration, with a referral agency acting as the 'stable third' in our therapeutic triangle. Our approach provides a coherent framework within which to integrate systemic practice with a focus on safety.

Our aim in establishing Reading Safer Families was to provide an affordable, independent specialist project within the local community, dedicated to working towards safety in family members' relationships. In the range of responses to family violence, we believed that we could make a contribution and work alongside men's groups, hostel work, couples' work, individual work, and so on. We offer risk assessment, therapeutic rehabilitation in the aftermath of violence and intervention to prevent further violence. We work with a wide range of violent relationships, including parents who are violent to their children, men who are violent to their women partners, women who are violent in their intimate relationships, adolescents and adult children who are violent to their older parents, adult carers who are violent to older people whom they look after and adult siblings who continue to be violent to each other into adulthood (Vetere and Cooper, 2001b). Our decision to establish an independent project, in partnership with each other, was prompted by our career-long wish to develop our thinking and skills further by keeping a focus on domestic violence in intimate and family relationships. In the past, we have both had experiences with employers who would not tolerate such a dedicated use of our clinical time. The irony for us is that, once having established ourselves as an independent trading agency, we found that former employers were only too pleased to buy back our services in this way.

In approaching our work in a focused way, there were a number of recurrent questions. The first question was: 'Should every therapist and practitioner working with family members ask about domestic violence and safety?' Our answer would be that they should, and that the implications for agency responses should be met, not least by developing a domestic violence policy. In our project, establishing a domestic violence policy and getting to grips with the problems of definition were our first tasks. We write more about this in Chapter 1, but suffice it to say here that we did not have the protection of an established agency for our work, so we needed to think carefully about how we could be seen to be accountable for our practice, and in putting safety first.

Our second compelling question was: 'How can we understand why some men are violent to their intimate partners and family, and some are not?' Systemic thinking helps us keep separate the moral, legal and psychological discourses around men's violence, while keeping their connections in mind (Goldner et al., 1990). The systemic field as such has not attempted to explain why we behave violently; rather our efforts have been rooted in describing intergenerational patterns of relationship, behaviour, meaning and context. At the same time, the pro-feminist stance is not without its problems (Vetere and Cooper, 2004). If we follow the logic of the argument, it is held that men learn abusive ways of behaving and develop a sense of entitlement to exert male privilege within a gendered, sexist society that reinforces patterns of abuse. The problem, however, becomes one of explanation and one of responsibility. The pro-feminist systemic analysis may well describe the putative relationship between entitlement beliefs and abusive behaviours, but to what extent can it explain why some men are violent and others not, why the worst of domestic violence is committed by a minority of men, and also why some women behave with violence, in both opposite-sex and same-sex relationships (Lie et al., 1991; Renzetti, 1992), given that we are all exposed at different times to similar cultural discourses? In our view, part of the problem lies with the experience of intimacy itself. We explore this further in the book, in particular in Chapter 2.

The limitations of a single argument response to this question have led some group intervention approaches for men who behave violently to develop the cognitive behavioural and pro-feminist model further, to include self-psychology, which is rooted in object relations thinking (Dunford, 2000; Wexler, 2000). Such an approach acknowledges the role of shame and shaming in men's lives, both as boys and as young men, and how identification with an abuser, in the absence of other emotional support, becomes a pattern of psychological survival for a child (Dutton, 2003). Later developments of the Duluth model actively incorporate such childhood experiences in group work with men (Graves, 1999). In our experience, recognition that a man has been harmed in his childhood does not, and need not, lessen his responsibility for harming others in his adulthood. Systemic thinking can help us keep these descriptions and responsibilities about safety in mind as well as allow us to ask about survival, resilience and potential for change (Goldner et al., 1990; Vetere and Cooper, 2004).

The third question in our thinking was: 'If men are sometimes victims of domestic violence, what services should be offered, and have we reached a point where this is politically and therapeutically acceptable?' Our clinical work and our reading have confirmed for us that men can sometimes be victims of violence in both heterosexual and same-sex intimate relationships, and that they are often reluctant to seek help. It is also worth considering that men can also be victims of violence from other men in social contexts outside intimate relationships. We are pleased to say that when 'Crossing Bridges', a partnership of Berkshire Women's Aid, Thames Valley Police and Reading Borough Council, opened in 2003, they described their service as one that 'can help you whether this is all new or has been happening for years, regardless of gender, age, sexuality, race, culture or religious belief'. In our view services for men should also focus on safety and should be part of a range of community-wide responses. We should be able to engage with and try to understand both men's and women's choices, whether or not we are in agreement: to stay, to leave, to come and go, to seek safety, to seek danger, to deal with fear, to take responsibility for their own and others' safety, to connect with their children safely as mothers and fathers, and all the rest of the messy complexity of working with violence in family life.

Some people might say that the rationale for working with men who behave with violence is essential to protect women and children now and in the future. We would extend the moral argument and assert that men are entitled to therapeutic services in their own right. Not to do so, and to tell the men that we provide a service to them only to keep women and children safe, potentially compromises the development of trust essential to any service or intervention offered. This would not help men develop a sense of confidence and self-respect, the lack of which often underlies abusive behaviour, alongside any felt entitlement to abuse those we love and live with in intimate relationships.

As systemic psychotherapists we wanted the creation of Reading Safer Families to give us an opportunity to develop our ideas about theory and practice in a way that was principled, pragmatic, personal and political. We are evolving a model of reflecting process that forms the basis for collaboration and transparency with our clients. We interview family members using a lead therapist and in-room consultant model that allows us to share the work equally and develop our ideas together and in the presence of our clients. We have developed our consultation process to include consideration of written texts, such as court reports, as well as spoken words. Descriptions and case examples of how we achieve this are included in the body of the book.

During the past eight years we have obviously learnt a great deal about developing a professional partnership in a difficult and complex area of work and in a culture where public discourse about violence in intimate relationships is often avoided or minimized and at worst is openly hostile. Initially we had links to two similar projects in Oxford and London, where we offered mutual consultation and support. However, there is no doubt that for some time our experience at Reading Safer Families was almost unique, but now the climate has changed positively and we increasingly encounter colleagues who work for agencies or public/private partnerships that actively encourage this dedicated use of their working time.

In writing this book we have paid attention to the reality that, in the development of any good partnership, there is always an element of fusion. As we both work in the room together in a reflecting process, over the last eight years we have observed, shaped and re-shaped the development of each other's therapeutic and consultative styles. Therefore, we write this book as two people who have been part of a most creative and inspirational partnership that has been formative in helping us both to construct our present sense of ourselves as therapists, trainers and writers. As we are both women and for ease of reading, we have used the convention of the feminine pronoun throughout the book.

We have regarded writing this book as an opportunity to expand further some of our knowledge and to develop new ideas in ways that have particularly interested us over the years by linking theory, our methodology and clinical experience plus case examples in a challenging way, e.g. Jan took her interest in language use and linguistics with her when she was a trainee at The Family Institute, Cardiff (1982–84). Her postgraduate diploma in Family Therapy dissertation was entitled, 'Not just words: An exploration of how women and men use language differently and the implications for family therapy' (unpublished dissertation). Since that time she has maintained her interest and attention to language in her teaching and practice. In the Reading Safer Families project the intersect of language use and the context of violent behaviour in intimate relationships creates interesting therapeutic dilemmas between words and action and can add new levels of meaning to the relationship patterns that we observe (Cooper, 1989). In addition, both Arlene and Jan have revisited an important earlier journey of understanding gender as a central analytic concept in our own world and the worlds of our clients (Vetere, 1992). We have reconsidered and expanded some of the influences of the feminist critique on systemic therapy and how a systemic therapist may now hold a 'multiversal' position on relative truths, as well as develop a moral and ethical basis for work with violence and safety.

We have written about our understanding of our specific use of reflective processes when trying to work for safety in family members' relationships. We have developed our ideas about working with the disabling effects of shame and blame, which we consider central to any therapist's work with domestic violence. Thinking about shame and blame as both nouns and verbs led us to consider further our ideas about the specific effects of legal and professional scrutiny, whether voluntary or involuntary, and their effects on both the family in their lived experience and the therapist in trying to understand the meaning of this in her particular context. The field of systemic therapy has been slower to recognize the importance of the therapeutic relationship and even slower to acknowledge the impact on the therapist of the therapeutic endeavour. Arlene's training in other models of psychotherapy, such as brief focal psychodynamic psychotherapy and models of cognitive–behavioural therapy, and our shared interest in attachment theory helped us explore some ideas about developing therapeutic relationships with people who perpetrate violence and who might behave defensively when 'sent' to therapy, the therapist's resilience against secondary traumatization, and the development of the personal and professional self of the therapist.

In this book we have continued to use the term 'domestic violence' as in all our other writings. We are aware that 'domestic violence' masks the issue of gender but we continue to use this description because it is most commonly used, it is the term used in most of the literature, and for us it can be used broadly to cover all kinds of family relationships, both residential and non-residential, where one person behaves violently towards another. We have used the terms 'father' and 'mother' to refer to the men and women who care for children in their own homes, even though the relationships may be diverse, e.g. step relationships, kin carers, foster carers, and so on. We include discussion on the impact and meaning of culture and issues to do with race, class, poverty and illiteracy where appropriate.

A number of research studies have made the link between sexual abuse of children and violence to partners (Frude, 1991; Farmer and Owen, 1995; Hester et al., 2000). Similarly, violence to partners is seen as a common context for child abuse (Moffitt and Caspi, 1998). Historically these links became somewhat lost in the subsequent debates around issues of practice and agency responses to child sexual abuse. However, although we acknowledge these important links, for the purposes of this book we shall focus on issues of domestic violence not on issues of sexual abuse as such. In our domestic violence project over the last eight years our referrals have mostly been concerned with men's violence in heterosexual couples. However, we have developed our ideas about understanding the differences between men's and women's violent behaviour within heterosexual couples and we have also worked with lesbian and gay couples.

Outline of the book

The book is divided into eight chapters which describe both theory and clinical practice. Chapter 1 is an introduction to Reading Safer Families' approach to risk assessment and risk management and outlines our systemic way of working and our focus on safety. Chapter 2 continues our discussion on risk assessment and risk management, by outlining our policy on confidentiality and how we develop our 'stable third' relationship with our referrers. It includes a description of how we create and maintain contracts of no violence. Chapter 3 shows how we use multiple theories within a systemic approach to practice, situated within a critical feminist framework. We introduce the importance of language use and linguistic research in our clinical work and report writing around family violence. Chapter 4 deals specifically with our particular use of reflecting processes. Chapter 5 outlines the impact of domestic violence on children and the implications for practice. Chapter 6 deals with issues for adults as victims, perpetrators and childhood witnesses. We discuss theoretical and practice ideas for working clinically with issues of shame and blame in current and past relationships. Chapter 7 addresses accountability and responsibility and the experiences of families in the court system. Chapter 8 considers the emotional impact of doing this type of work on practitioners and draws some implications for the supervision of practitioners working with domestic violence. Finally, we close the book with our reflections on the importance of a safety focus and look towards future work. We use examples from our practice as points of illustration. We have tried to use examples that illustrate how diverse people approach some common problems in intimate living when violence is of concern.

Jan Cooper
Arlene Vetere

Acknowledgements

This book is dedicated to all the clients with whom we have worked over the years and who have taught us with generosity and struggled so hard to escape the cycles of violence.

Jan would like to thank her partner David Cooper, who has always kept his curiosity about systems thinking and who has been so supportive over the years. Thanks also to Nicholas, Robert and Emmeline, including Jo and Mathias, whose interest has always energised her.

We would like to say a special thank you to Graham McManus, whose hard work and support helped to create Reading Safer Families. Our thanks go also to Alistair Keddie, Consultant Clinical Psychologist, Head of Clinical Psychology Services, Berkshire Healthcare Trust, for his personal encouragement and his bold professional commitment to our project.

Our thanks go to John Hills for his help with a careful reading of the manuscript.

In using clinical material, we have sought permission where possible and changed names and other details to protect anonymity.

CHAPTER 1

Family violence and the systemic approach to interventions

Approaches to the definition of violent behaviour

Our first task in setting up a domestic violence service was to choose a definition that would encompass our therapeutic and assessment work with families. Our understanding of violence in family relationships was broad and included physical violence, sexual abuse, neglect, emotional abuse and other psychological abuse, including coercion, intimidation and verbal abuse (O'Leary and Jouriles, 1994; Humphries et al., 2001). We adopted the Council of Europe's Council of Ministers' definition because it invites us to think about the intentions behind acts that harm family members or fail to protect others from significant harm, highlighting the different responsibilities around safety in family relationships (Vetere and Cooper, 2003). In addition, the definition recognizes that significant harm has its effects in the broader context of psychological development, and thus is pertinent to the effects on children of witnessing violence between family members. The Council of Europe (1986) definition is as follows:

> Any act or omission committed within the framework of the family, by one of its members that undermines the life, the bodily or psychological integrity, or the liberty of another member of the same family, or that seriously harms the development of his or her personality.

We find this definition helpful for the following reasons:

- It invites us to think about responsibility for safety alongside responsibility for acts that harm others.
- It recognizes that acts of violence have psychological and relational impacts that are iterative over time.
- It recognizes that acts of violence may be both historical and ongoing.
- It recognizes that acts of violence that might otherwise be defined as less severe, such as pushing or shoving, are important in terms of their putative effects.

1

- Implicit in the definition of ensuing harm is the recognition of issues of power and control in acts of violence.

Our definition has been important to us in maintaining our framework and clarity of thought. We also use it in training and organizational consultancy and from time to time solicitors have written asking for our definition either to use in court or to assist them in writing instructions that will appropriately attend to relational family issues around domestic violence and risk and safety.

Since the publication of the Council of Europe's definition of violence in the family, the World Health Assembly (WHA) (1996) 'declared violence as a priority in public health' (Resolution WHA 49.25) and 'called upon member states of the United Nations to eliminate violence against women and children' (Resolution WHA 50.19). The World Health Organization (WHO) Task Force on Violence and Health (WHO, 2000) declared its four priorities to be:

1. To define and characterize different types of violence and assess the consequences;
2. To understand the causes of violence and identify risk factors for aggressive behaviour;
3. To identify best practice and evaluate interventions aimed at preventing violence;
4. To strengthen the capacity of the health and social systems to disseminate knowledge and implement programmes to reduce violence in society, especially that directed at women and children.

We support these declarations, but would have wished to see men included in this thinking, because they can be at risk of harm in intimate relationships, e.g. in same-sex relationships, and from homicide, however motivated. Men are most often seen in the legal system, and responded to within the legal system. Alongside this, we believe that men are entitled to therapeutic services in their own right, provided that this treatment is not done in isolation from other family, community and professional responses, and pays attention to safety as the first priority. Although this book is about family-based violence and family safety, we do have concerns that, of all of us, young men are most at risk of violence outside their homes. Mostly they will be living at home, so the effects of their attacks on others, and others' attacks on them, will be felt within the family system and will form part of the context of violence in our culture.

Although our work covers a wide range of violent acts, within different family and intimate relationships, we are influenced also by the more narrowly focused definitions of domestic violence, i.e. violence from one intimate partner to another, used within different agencies and government departments within the UK, e.g. the Home Office for England uses the following definition:

> . . . the term 'domestic violence' shall be understood to mean any violence between current and former partners in an intimate relationship, wherever and whenever the violence occurs. The violence may include physical, sexual, emotional and financial abuse.
>
> Blunkett (2003)

This definition has been adopted by all police authorities in England and Wales, and yet it is interesting to note that the corresponding Crown Prosecution Service (CPS, 2001) has adopted a different definition of domestic violence:

> Any criminal offence arising out of physical, sexual, psychological, emotional or financial abuse by one person against a current or former partner in a close relationship, or against a current or former family member.

A number of important implications arise from these interagency definitional differences, such as exclusion of certain people or situations from help, or even failure to protect those for whom the definitions are designed to protect, such as, in the first definition, where only partners are defined as perpetrators.

The extent and seriousness of the problem

> People are more likely to be killed, physically assaulted, hit, beaten up, slapped or spanked in their own homes by other family members than anywhere else, or by anyone else in our society.
>
> Gelles and Cornell (1990)

The British Crime Survey (1996) reported that about 30 per cent of violent crime was domestic assault, with 90 per cent of women surveyed reporting attacks from their male partners, and 48 per cent of men reporting attacks from their female partners. In one-third of these attacks, the attacker was reported to be using drugs and/or alcohol. Differences in the frequency and severity of the men's attacks on the women were recorded, with greater injury and psychological upset experienced by the women victims. It could be argued that, as men know the effects of their violent actions will be greater, this changes the assessment of the intent of men's violence. Twenty-three per cent of women and 15 per cent of men aged 16–59 interviewed in the 2000 British Crime Survey reported an attack from a current or ex-partner, and 12 per cent of those women and 5 per cent of those men were assaulted on more than three occasions. Although some US research purports to show similar rates of violent behaviour within heterosexual couples (Wilson and Daly, 1992), other research would suggest that women are more likely to behave aggressively in self-defence (Saunders, 1986; Dobash et al., 1992). It is of interest to us that duration of the attacks is not recorded within most of the demographic research studies. Despite the obvious problems of subjective experiences of time and how that may be affected when under severe duress, we find the length of an attack to be an important factor when assessing for safety, and for motivation to change in the male perpetrator. In our clinical work, we also meet women who report being held captive within their own homes, or too frightened to emerge from a place of hiding, such as a bathroom.

The United Nations' Statistical Office (WHO, 2000) estimated that 28 per cent of women in the USA had been attacked by an intimate partner in the last year; similarly 25 per cent of women in Belgium, 25 per cent of women in Norway and 17 per cent of women in New Zealand. Straus and Gelles (1990) estimated that one in eight women in the USA was physically assaulted by her male partner each year, and at least one in three women was assaulted over the lifetime of her relationship. In addition, they point out that women are more at risk of assault and murder during the period of separation and divorce from a previously violent male partner, especially during contact handover arrangements with children and during pregnancy. This raises the issue of assault on the unborn child. The variation in the reported incidence and prevalence of violent attacks on women by their men partners, both within and across countries, is largely thought to be a problem of under-reporting, differences in the definitions of violent behaviour used in some studies, and different means of collecting information, such as telephone survey, face-to-face interview, police records, and so on.

In comparison to the body of data recording and estimating a man's violence towards his woman partner, there is very little research done with lesbian and gay couples. This lack of psychological research has implications for the slower development of legal protections for same-sex couples and may contribute to a myth that same-sex couple violence is not a problem. Island and Letellier (1991) writing in the USA express concern that the majority of cases are never reported. Despite this relative lack of research, the existing literature has established that same-sex couple violence exists with equal prevalence to opposite-sex couple violence (Potoczniak et al., 2003). Turrell (2000) explored a variety of forms of violence, such as emotional, physical, sexual and financial, among a group of lesbian women, gay women and gay men (in the research the women could choose to self-define as either lesbian or gay). They found that 44 per cent of gay men, 58 per cent of gay women and 55 per cent of lesbian women reported being physically assaulted in a present or previous relationship. Lie and her colleagues (1991) worked with a sample of 170 lesbian women currently living with a woman partner – all were white, well educated, in their 30s and living in Arizona, USA. Of the women 120 indicated that they had either used aggression against a partner or been victimized by aggressive behaviour; 136 had had previous relationships with both men and women. The researchers found that the women reported higher rates of abuse from their women partners than from their men partners. This finding surprised the researchers, and they suggested that some aspect of the experience of intimacy with a partner may well play a role in initiating and explaining some aggressive behaviour in intimate relationships. A further study with lesbian women by Renzetti (1992) suggested that feelings of dependency and jealousy played a major role in the use of violent behaviour. We shall return to issues of intimacy and adult attachment later in this book, when thinking of how we develop explanations for why people behave violently in the context of relationship intimacy. Clearly, the feminist critiques of patriarchy and the practices of inequality have been helpful to therapists in thinking about the social and cultural contexts that promote and condone violent behaviour from men to their women partners (Pence and Paymar, 1993). If, however, all of us are subject to the same discourses around patriarchal entitlement, we need to explain what factors and experiences contribute to some of us behaving violently, in different relationships, more or less of the time, or not at all. Thus, when conducting our risk assessments in cases where violence is known to have taken place in a same-sex or opposite-sex couple, we draw distinctions between the different patterns and severities of violence, and explore carefully the concept of control behind the violence. We return to this issue at various places in this book.

Moffitt and Caspi (1998) estimated, from their review of the effects of domestic violence on children, that two-thirds of physical attacks were witnessed by children, and that children are at four to nine times greater risk of being assaulted themselves if they live in homes where their fathers hit their mothers. When considering parental violence towards children, under-reporting is similarly considered to be a problem by most commentators. The Department of Health for England (1995) estimated that 4 in 1000 children in the UK are included in the Child Protection Register, and are abused/neglected. However, the Department of Health for England (1995) also estimated that 9 of 10 children are hit by their parents, which could mean that abuse goes undetected. An American survey carried out with parents by Straus and Gelles (1986) estimated that 1 in 10 children aged between 3 and 17 was severely physically assaulted in the year 1985. Subsequent research done by this team found a reduction in reported rates of more serious assault, which led the researchers to speculate on the benefits of preventive public education campaigns. Browne and Herbert (1997), in their review of the research on interventions designed to prevent parent-to-child violence, concluded that interventions that strengthen the parent–child relationship are likely to be more effective than those interventions that focus on parental psychological problems alone. In this finding, we see the helpfulness of the systemic approach, which focuses on relationships, emotional attachments, the development of resilience and problem-solving abilities across the generational lifespan of family and kin groups.

Violence between siblings

Gelles and Cornell (1990) observed that the increased public awareness of the abuse of women and children in their own homes by partners/fathers has had the unanticipated consequence of people assuming that these are the most problematic aspects of violence in the home. Frude (1991) points out that sibling violence is very common, and that it is often perceived as 'normal'. It raises an interesting question for us about what is considered to be violent behaviour (and therefore unacceptable?) among siblings, such as pushing, shoving, pinching, hair pulling, etc., and how the context in which this behaviour occurs determines how meaning is ascribed to the behaviour, alongside what else the children might be observing and learning from the adults who have responsibility for their care. We have worked with a number of men who behave violently towards their women partners, who describe sibling relationships in their childhoods that we would consider to range from bullying to violently assaultative, although they would not – they would often see the behaviour as normal sibling rivalry. Bullying has been defined by Lane (1989) as 'any action or implied action, such as threats of violence, intended to cause fear or distress' more than once. There are no data to help us estimate rates of bullying between siblings, but, if we look to schools within the UK, there are some suggestions that rates of bullying between children are high, e.g. Ahmad and Smith (1989), in their survey of 2000 students in middle and senior schools, have estimated an incidence of 1 in 5 children being bullied and 1 in 10 children doing the bullying. Estimates of those who 'stand by' and do not intervene are not available. Steinmetz (1977) studied sibling conflict in American families and remarked on the difficulties of gaining parental cooperation with her research – not because the parents were uncooperative but because they did not see their children's aggressive behaviour to each other as problematic, considered it normal, and were often too busy to discriminate between incidents in terms of severity, and so on. Similarly, Dunn (1996), working in England, observed sibling interactions at home, on two occasions 6 months apart. She reported that the research team observed a high rate of sibling arguments, on average about eight quarrels an hour. The mother's intrusion into the arguments was correlated with higher rates of conflict at the later visit, compared with those mothers who ignored the arguments combined with rewarding the children for not engaging in conflict. In addition, she concluded, from her review of the research on parental intervention and non-intervention in sibling arguments, that parents need to point out to their children, when young, the consequences of aggressive action, if they are to help their children learn to care about what happens to others.

In thinking about the implications of the above findings for practitioners who work with children and families across the lifespan, we wish to return to the question of whether we routinely ask about violent behaviour in relationships and in the home. The findings of two American studies pose challenges to our practice. Straus (1994) found that two-thirds of clients in couples/family meetings had engaged in physical violence against their partner in the year before the start of therapy. Similarly, Ehrensaft and Vivian (1996) found that 60 per cent of couples seeking couples' therapy had behaved aggressively towards their partners but only 10 per cent spontaneously reported this to their counsellors. Ehrensaft and Vivian went on to ask why the couples did not report it, and why the counsellors did not ask. The couples said that there were many reasons, e.g. perceiving physical violence as trivial or tolerable, violence was not the 'real' problem, wanting to make a good impression, shame and humiliation, fear and risk of further victimization, love and concern for the partner, and violent behaviour seen to be a learned way of resolving conflict, whereas the counsellors said they did not ask because it was not part of their assessment procedures. It would be interesting to repeat the research now, to try to see what changes might have come about in assessment practices as a result of increased awareness of the prevalence of violent behaviour.

Risk, responsibility and collaboration

In our work, we make a distinction between the assessment of risk and the management of risk when violent behaviour is known to have occurred, whether we are doing assessment work for the courts, or for therapeutic work and family reunification. In this section, we outline some of the issues that occur regularly regarding the assessment of risk and the management of risk, and how we developed our ideas about safety in relationships. The three themes of risk, responsibility and collaboration are continually interwoven into our thinking when working with family members. We develop these themes whether working therapeutically, for assessment of risk, consultation or rehabilitation.

Risk

A continuous programme of risk assessment is part of our strategic approach to risk management. Some of the families and family members with whom we work have been assessed by other agencies, e.g. forensic psychology and psychiatry services, probation services, when a family member has been sent to prison for violent behaviour, or social workers and expert witnesses in child protection cases. These families have often been through a lengthy legal process and are subject to intense and stressful scrutiny (Vetere and Cooper, 2001b). We carry out our own risk assessments as a precursor to any therapeutic work, whether or not it has been recommended by other professionals. This is not to say that we ignore the findings of others, but rather we recognize that past violent behaviour can be said to predict future violent behaviour, and continuous assessment allows us to proceed with caution. We usually devote at least six sessions to a court assessment of further risk of violent behaviour before we proceed with family reunification plans, or any other form of therapeutic work. During this time, we engage our clients in a no-violence contract and help them develop safety in their relationships. We discuss no-violence contracting in further detail in Chapter 2. In our experience, stopping the violence can be achieved, but what tests and challenges us, as therapists, is helping couples and family members untangle the complex social and psychological legacy of violent behaviour for their intimate relating once the violent behaviour has stopped.

The 'stable third'

We undertake assessments of risks of violence, or of further violence following conviction or child care proceedings, and therapeutic rehabilitation with families in the aftermath of violent behaviour. We receive therapy referrals from NHS trusts, Social Services, probation services and the courts. We do not accept referrals directly from the general public. This is part of our risk management strategy. We form a triangle with the family, the referring agency and ourselves, with the referring agency acting as our 'third'.

When it is known by professional workers that violent behaviour has occurred within family relationships, most people respond with anxiety that it will or may occur again. For us, understanding and working with the different sources and manifestations of anxiety for family members, professional workers and their agencies are crucial to our approach to risk management, e.g. if family reunification is recommended by the courts, we all take risks – ourselves, the family members, and the professional workers and their agencies. None of our cases has been without risk. In our practice, we use regular reviews, at the start of the assessment period, and during both the assessment and the therapeutic work to identify the risks taken by each of the three positions in our risk assessment triangle. For many of the couples and families with whom we have worked, they are not used to taking part in such three-way review meetings, where risks are identified for all and strategies developed to reduce risk and manage anxiety. We write about our reviewing process further in Chapters 2 and 3.

These ongoing meetings with our referrers and other professionals working with the couple/family maintain our basic sustainable network. Not only was it that as an independent project we were not protected by working within a large agency, because some agencies do have policies of domestic violence anyway, but also it was that we had to set our own boundaries and limitations around what we could and could not do in the context of risk and risk assessment (Vetere and Cooper, 2001b, 2003). This basic sustainable network allows us to develop working relationships with referrers based on trust and accountability and corroboration of what family members may tell us. In the early days of our project, the attention paid to the referrer was crucial to our acceptance in the local professional network both by referrers and within the legal network. In this way it is common knowledge that some form of domestic violence has been talked about between the client and the professional before referral to us. Our dedication to working with domestic violence is, therefore, clear from the outset and we talk about the referrers' concerns in our first meeting. In addition, we belong to our local domestic violence forum, organized by Women's Aid, as another way of keeping informed and maintaining our network of professional relationships. We discuss how we develop and maintain our relationships with our referrers further in Chapter 2.

Under-reporting and minimization of violent behaviour continues to be a concern. Dobash and Dobash (1992) estimate from their survey of police records in Glasgow and Edinburgh that only 2 of 98 physical assaults on women by their male partners were reported to the police. In addition we know that many research-based definitions of physical violence do not include pushing and shoving as a source of psychological distress (Vetere and Cooper, 1999). We can of course keep under-reporting in mind as we work and we will often hear new disclosures during the work. However, the way in which we can talk about domestic violence, in a straightforward way, is crucial, in our view, to a successful piece of work.

Thus, in addition to our basic sustainable network we require everyone involved to share joint responsibility for the risks involved, for accepting responsibility for their actions and for developing collaboration and cooperation while the work is in progress. As we say above, we discuss these issues with our clients when we meet them. Quite often we meet clients who do not imagine that we or Social Services, for example, will be taking risks on their behalf.

The contexts of violence and repeat violence

We pay particular attention to how much is known about the context in which violence occurred and the frequency, severity and duration of the violence, e.g. did the violence occur in the context of family living and/or did it occur at work, with colleagues or socially, with friends and acquaintances, including sporting activities? Did the violent behaviour include violence towards property and objects and the use of weapons? Is the threat of violence maintained by other means, such as intimidation? Does living in the 'goldfish bowl' of others' scrutiny make a difference? Such questioning provides information on people's understanding of social roles and rules and social rule violations, and their sense of entitlement to use physical means to get their own way (Vetere and Cooper, 2001b). We combine our opportunities to repeat such questions with our own observations. Can the perpetrator of violence manage his frustration, irritation and anger when talking to us, or when talking to his woman partner in front of us? Does he try to control and intimidate us? For example, one man we interviewed for a court assessment insisted on calling his wife a 'dirty lesbian' despite us making it clear we would not tolerate hearing any negative comments about others, either family members or professional workers.

Use and misuse of psychoactive substances

We assess for the use and misuse of psychoactive substances. If there is a problem we help with a referral to our community alcohol and drugs teams, and we expect to work in collaboration with these services. We find that we can support our commitment to abstinence or controlled drinking within our work, and may include the substance misuse key worker in our reviewing process, where appropriate. We know of other practitioners who prefer to wait until the alcohol/drug problem has been sorted out but our experience teaches us that we can work concurrently with our alcohol/drugs services colleagues if we establish clear and regular liaison.

Empathy

We attend to signs of empathy or lack of empathy for the person harmed by the violence, and pay careful attention to descriptions and observations of negative empathy, i.e. exploiting a victim's vulnerability to inflict further psychological harm. We are looking for signs and descriptions that demonstrate an emotional congruence rather than a cognitive ability to talk about how a child or woman partner might be fearful as the perpetrator looms over her, for example. We are informed by the work of Jacobson and Gottman (1998) and others, which describes how some violent men act in cool, instrumental and controlling ways; this compares to the flat emotional responses and use of exaggerated control techniques described by Hare (1993) in his work on psychopathy. Dobash et al. (1999) and Dunford (2000) comment on the inability and often the unwillingness of violent men to reflect on their violence and its consequences. In the Dobash et al. (1999) evaluation study of British programmes for violent men, they noted that men who completed a programme successfully developed the ability to think about their violence and its costs to themselves, their partners, their children and others. We pursue the notion of self-reflexivity in our work with family members who behave violently to one another, and see our job as trying to help them develop further their abilities to self-reflect. Fonagy and Target (1997), using attachment theory ideas, describe this process as reflective self-functioning – the ability to look back on positive and negative emotional experiences, to process the experience and develop the meanings, for both oneself and others for whom one has moral and emotional responsibilities, now and in the future.

Internal motivation for change

Where there appears to be little internal motivation for change in relationships and that motivation does not seem to develop over a period of continuous assessment, but rather seems to be a result of externally induced motivation for change (e.g. by statutory or legal agencies), we are highly unlikely to undertake therapeutic work for rehabilitation. Where there is some internal motivation to change, we try to enhance a person's motivation and intention to stop behaving aggressively by using motivational interviewing methods (Miller and Rollnick, 1991). We have adapted these methods to be both systemic and suitable for working with family members who behave violently, e.g. helping the man express concerns about a need to change, or helping the development of a resolution to take action. We use past and future questions to contrast hopes and aspirations for behaviour between then and now. We use the comparisons to explore the costs, the benefits, and the importance of current behavioural choices for them, their relationships and their futures (Vetere and Cooper, 2000, 2001a, 2001b). We explore thoughts and feelings of ambivalence towards change by asking how life might be after violent behaviour stops, by exploring differences between the ideal self and the actual self, and exploring their developing concerns for themselves, their partners, their children and other family members.

These approaches to asking questions can be helpful in reducing defensiveness and facilitating therapeutic engagement. In particular, we have found that, if we ask questions in role, it helps people stay thoughtful while responding to challenging questions about their violent behaviour. So, for example, we might ask a man who has behaved violently towards his woman partner, in his role as a father, what he thinks his sons and daughters are learning from him about how men treat women, or what he hopes his children can learn from him, or how he teaches his sons and daughters to keep themselves safe, now and in future partnerships of their own. We might ask him what he would recommend to his son if he seeks help about managing his own temper, or what he will tell his sons and daughters about this particular violent incident when they get older?

In summary, then, we work with safety in relationships as our first priority, before we agree to consider broader therapeutic aspects of the work with a couple or other family relationship. We agree a safety plan with our referrers and the couple during our initial meetings; this includes a place of safety for women and children if needed, e.g. at a Women's Aid hostel, and an agreed network of informed and helpful professional, community and extended family members who will support the safety work. Often our work with a couple is one part of a safety plan that includes other interventions.

Responsibility

We have been influenced by the work of Goldner and colleagues at the Ackerman Institute (Goldner et al., 1990; Jenkins, 1990; Jory et al., 1997; Goldner, 1998, 1999; Jory and Anderson, 1999) in their attempts to hold the tension in therapeutic work between the responsibility for violent behaviour, on the one hand, and explanation for violence, on the other, in such a way that the explanation is not used by the perpetrator to minimize or deny his violent intent and action. In our assessment we look for some acknowledgement that there is a problem, accountability for behaviour, responsibility for keeping oneself and others safe, and a recognition of how relational factors may contribute to the problem, without recourse to the consistent blaming of others. We do not proceed with any therapeutic or rehabilitation work if we do not hear and see responsible talk and responsible behaviour in action. We listen in detail to how a perpetrator of violence describes his violent actions, because everyday language can hide and minimize what happened, e.g. if a man tells us he 'just shoved' his partner, we will ask both what the 'shove' looked like, and what the 'just' means. We discuss issues of language in therapeutic work further in Chapter 3.

The parenting assessment and risk management procedures developed by Reder and Lucey (1995) and Fitzpatrick (1995), in the context of child protection, are helpful to us because they similarly emphasize the different aspects of accountability and responsibility. In particular they highlight the importance of showing and sustaining an ability to see professionals as potentially helpful to them and their families, and to cooperating with statutory services. In our experience this is hard for many families, who may hold beliefs about not discussing 'family business' with 'outsiders', or who see the world as a hostile place in response to their own childhood experiences of abuse and rarely give their trust to others, and/or who have been subject to intense scrutiny and occasional inconsistency on the part of those professionals with responsibility for overseeing child protection procedures. For example, we worked with a family who had lived under scrutiny from Social Services and whose children had been regularly reviewed for over 11 years and had believed they were doing 'good enough'. The arrival of a new social worker, with a different understanding of what constitutes 'good enough' parenting, paved the way for court procedures that left the father feeling angry and hostile and the mother feeling like giving up. However hard such scrutiny may be, we believe the ability of parents to sustain their commitment to cooperation with professionals is at the heart of successful family reunification.

Thus, the development of personal and parental agency around safety and problem-solving in the aftermath of violence is part of our approach to risk management. We ask questions to encourage the couple to think about the effects of violence on their children. Developing the couple's own sense of agency for problem-solving around their own relationship, responsibility for safety and their relationship with their children is the plank on which we build a rehabilitation plan and on which getting their children back from the care of Social Services may depend (Vetere and Cooper, 1999, 2001a, 2001b). Since we began our domestic violence work in the Reading Safer Families project, we have been part of a sea change in attitudes in UK statutory services to the assessment of risks to children who 'witness' parental violence.

Collaboration

We aim to be as transparent as we can in our therapeutic and rehabilitative work with family members. Thus, we are clear with them about our own moral position around the use of violence in family relationships, our use of social control procedures and our use of reflecting processes (Smith and Kingston, 1980; Andersen, 1987; Friedman, 1995). We try always to be clear about the differences between the responsibility for violent actions and the explanations for those actions, such that explanation cannot easily be used to diminish responsibility. We write about these dilemmas further in Chapter 3. Our policy on confidentiality is discussed in Chapter 2 and we develop our ideas on reflecting processes in Chapter 4.

We are accountable for our work in a number of ways:

1. We evaluate our therapeutic outcomes during our work and immediately after our work has been completed, by seeking verbal feedback from our clients, referrers and other professionals where appropriate. Our regular review meetings are the main vehicle for giving and receiving feedback, including ideas for how we might have been more helpful. We try to involve our clients in thinking with us at strategic service levels to facilitate their ideas in how we provide a service to future clients. We offer 'top-up' work when we think it is needed and when we are asked. We try to offer an 'open door' policy, so that people are able to return to us should the need arise.

2. We make use of different theoretical approaches when trying to explain violent behaviour and its setting conditions, both past and present. We integrate ideas that we and our clients find helpful within an ongoing process of systemic formulation (Vetere and Dallos, 2003). These ideas are available for scrutiny and interrogation from the different perspectives within our therapeutic triangle (ourselves, our clients and our referrers).

3. From a moral relational standpoint, we think the ability to take responsibility for violent behaviour and to hold ourselves accountable for what we do and the consequences for others and our relationships to be the highest context marker for our therapeutic work. This position is, of course, inclusive of us. At times, we may well use self-disclosure to help further illuminate a particular moral dilemma, and to facilitate the development of therapeutic relationships that are not based on the notion that we might somehow inhabit the moral high ground or have found all the right answers in our own lives!

4. We will collaborate and work alongside other professionals as best we can, attending their review meetings where possible, such that our practice is open to professional scrutiny and evaluation.

CHAPTER 2

Family safety and the therapeutic process

Policy on confidentiality

We do not offer confidentiality in our work with families in the aftermath of violence or where violent behaviour is suspected; rather we negotiate confidentiality on a continuous basis where appropriate. This takes a step beyond our normal duty of care as practitioners, where we offer confidentiality except in circumstances where we think someone is at risk of harm, or of doing harm. We explain our policy of no confidentiality to people when we first meet them, along with the safety and risk management implications of our position (Vetere and Cooper, 2001b). If we are worried that someone is at risk from harm or likely to harm others, we tell family members that we will inform the appropriate statutory and legal authorities. We will try to discuss our concerns with them before informing others, but we will not offer confidentiality around these concerns. Carpenter and Treacher (1989) suggested that the two main reasons why practitioners may not discuss their concerns around suspected violence with adult family members are:

(1) fear of losing the perpetrator from therapy; combined with
(2) fear that the victim of violence will suffer reprisals as a result of initiating discussion.

Clearly this has implications for the practice of therapy supervisors, and we discuss this further in Chapter 8. Thus, for us, if a woman confides during an individual meeting about her partner's violent behaviour towards her, we do not force disclosure in the couple's meeting if we consider that unprepared disclosure will place the woman at further risk. However, we do explore issues of risk and safety with her partner in an individual meeting with him, using our risk assessment approach. If we cannot gain any therapeutic leverage in this meeting or engagement with issues of safety, we continue to discuss safety strategies with the woman, and ways to involve the statutory services. We had thought initially that our stance on 'no confidentiality' would offend and dissuade people from using our service. Instead it seems to have had the opposite effect, in that, when we ask our clients for feedback, they tell us that they are pleased to know where they stand with us and that they find us straightforward in our approach (Vetere and Cooper, 2001b). This position of 'no confidentiality' also allows statutory and voluntary agencies to trust us and rely on our practice when they employ us or liaise with us in therapeutic or assessment work.

We do not attempt therapy or rehabilitation with family members whom we believe to be at higher risk of further violence. When working with couples, for example, there needs to be an agreement that both partners wish for and are committed to finding a way to live together safely, e.g. we would not work therapeutically with a couple where the woman is afraid to meet or be in the room with her male partner. Nor would we work therapeutically with a family that included children and young people, until we were satisfied that the parents or carers were able to take responsibility for the children's safety. Bograd and Mederos (1999) suggest that a woman's willingness to discuss her partner's violence in his presence is an important indicator of whether a conjoint treatment approach is possible.

This position of 'no confidentiality', of course, challenges conventional family and couples' therapy ideas that a therapist's neutrality is compromised by secrets. It also supports the conventional feminist criticism of the use of neutrality in family therapy where the therapist listens in an even-handed way to all views as part of a systemic understanding and regards them all as equally important (Bograd and Mederos, 1999). Burck and Daniel (1995, p. 63) make the following comment:

> It is extremely difficult to remain neutral in the face of violence, and it is unethical to be neutral to the act itself.

They quote Wiesel (1989) who said 'neutrality helps the oppressor, never the victim'. It is our opinion that it is also unethical to remain neutral in thinking about the effects and complexity of domestic violence on family and intimate relationships. By taking a determined stand on issues of confidentiality we have been true to our own principles and encouraged transparency in the wider professional system. In our court reports we write about our practice of 'no confidentiality', and so in our spoken words and written texts our ideas are compatible.

We are often asked how we would know if people were lying to us. In our thinking, lying has its consequences, e.g. if we observe clients who are too interested in their own performance, engage in extreme impression management, or display consistent/marked discrepancies in their verbal reports or between their verbal and non-verbal behaviour, or if there are discrepancies between their verbal accounts and the written reports of others, we proceed with caution and question systemically around the effects of what we are noticing. In addition, we make use of cognitive interview procedures, developed by Geiselman and Fisher (1988), to help eye witnesses remember events. We agree with them that maintaining lies is more difficult under the combined conditions of:

- context reinstatement: get a picture in your mind and report everything you can
- change the order of events: recount the story in a different temporal order
- change the perspective: what would a third person see if she was there?

We interview and continuously assess over time as part of our risk management approach. Therefore, we never offer fewer than six sessions for court assessments or therapeutic work. In this way we have the advantage of looking for consistency in explanations and descriptions and in exploring the positive potential for change over time (Vetere and Cooper, 2001b).

Relationship with referrers – the stable third

Our referrers can be from social services, probation, the courts, general practice and our local NHS trust. We do not accept referrals directly from the general public. We knew at an early stage of the project that we wanted to think strategically and systemically about the assessment *and* management of risk when working therapeutically with rehabilitation. Thus, we recruit our referrers into our risk-management strategy, whereby all three participating groups – ourselves, the family members and the referrer(s) and their management system – understand and state the risks for all of us involved in any reunification plan. We all meet regularly, normally before the first session and after every fourth to sixth session, to review the progress of the work. These reviews are used to understand the risks involved from each of the three perspectives, to plan strategically to help manage the risks and to progress the rehabilitation work once safety has been prioritized.

In terms of risk management, our referrers act as our stable third, and we act as theirs, in understanding and coping with the anxieties generated by reunification and therapeutic work in the aftermath of violent behaviour. Our referrers can be the stable third for our clients in their relationship with us. Most importantly, the referrers offer another point of view, which may corroborate what the family members are telling us or challenge what we are being told. This stable third position also requires collaboration and cooperation and as a process is helpful in managing anxiety within family and professional systems. Ideally, our referrer would be well known to the family members, and may well visit the home on a regular basis. Thus, a health visitor or social worker, faith leader or community worker, and sometimes family practitioners, can be well placed to act as the stable third in our therapeutic triangle. If our referrer is not well known to the family and cannot corroborate what we are being told, we always negotiate for an alternative professional or voluntary worker to complement the existing role of our referrer. We have described here the minimum therapeutic triangle necessary for our work, but often we are involved in a series of interlocking triangular relationships because many of the families with whom we work have multiple relationships within many agencies, the staff of which sometimes do not communicate well across interagency boundaries. Our systemic approach helps us conceptualize these complex systems and how we fit within them, and promotes systemic thinking within family and professional review meetings, convened by either us or others in the course of their work (Vetere and Cooper, 2001b).

Assessment for therapy

In putting safety first, we make a clear distinction between assessment and therapy. Even if people come to us with forensic risk assessments, we still insist on doing our own risk assessment for therapeutic work. Our general approach is somewhat similar to the Ackerman couples and domestic violence project (Goldner et al., 1990; Goldner, 1999), whereby they did not work with couples in their project unless they could be violence free. During assessment and therapy, we talk to family members separately and together. We notice discrepancies in accounts and discrepancies between what people say and what they are observed to do. However, this is not to say that we expect coherence and consistency all the time, because incoherence and inconsistency can be said to characterize everyday discourse. However, we notice in particular discrepancies between written reports and verbal accounts. Thus, we would not convene the children until we were convinced that the parents could take responsibility for their violent behaviour, and develop their responsibilities and problem-solving around their children's well-being. For this reason, we proceed slowly with assessment for engagement in therapeutic work, i.e. assessment of the ability to take responsibility for violent behaviour and the ability to take safety seriously – one's own and that of others for whom one has responsibility (Vetere and Cooper, 2001a, 2001b).

We engage clients in a no-violence contract at the start of the work, and whether we are working with adult-to-adult violence, adult-to-child violence or grown up child-to-adult violence, we try to create a context of accountability for the perpetrator and a context of safety for the victim (Jory et al., 1997; Vetere and Cooper, 2001b). As we say elsewhere in this book, the key issue for us is in helping people take responsibility for their violent behaviour, and in developing responsibility for safety in relationships, while trying to understand how violent behaviour happens, without the explanation diluting responsibility! For example, when first working with a man and his violent behaviour towards his female partner, we follow the approach of Jory et al. (1997):

- To develop an awareness of how his violent actions and attitudes of entitlement to be violent affect his partner's well-being and impact on their relationship.
- To begin to question his motives for violent action, and to appreciate the complexity of his motivation.
- To begin to explore different ways of thinking about the entitlement to behave violently, and about day-to-day dilemmas of living that may act as triggers for violent behaviour.
- To point out alternative options and courses of responsible action in response to these day-to-day dilemmas.
- To acknowledge and begin to explore experiences of abuse in his family of origin, and other social settings, and from where his attitudes of entitlement to be violent may have originated and been inculcated.
- To discuss societal patterns that foster or condone abuse, such as racism, sexism, and so on.

We work hard to help people hold to their no-violence contracts, using behavioural, cognitive and other problem-solving methods to understand the triggers for violent behaviour and to develop safety strategies (see below for a fuller description). When we are fairly sure that the no-violence contract can be adhered to, and we have some external corroboration through our regular reviewing process, we widen the contract to include other coercive and psychologically abusive behaviours, whether they are self-defensive or otherwise retaliatory in origin. It is at this point that therapy proper could be said to begin as we move into the realm of family members' increased psychological vulnerability, when working with the legacy of violence, and the developmental and intergenerational origins of violent behaviour and attitudes to violence (Vetere and Cooper, 2001b).

When people come to us at Reading Safer Families, they are known to have been violent even though we might not know, or may never know, the extent of the violence. This is a major difference between ourselves and some colleagues who work in the private and public sector, where they may suspect domestic violence in the context of an intimate relationship, but that was not the focus of the referral to them. Geffner and Pagelow (1990) have written an informative and helpful list of questions that can be used by any practitioner who wishes to clarify with sensitivity the position of a woman or man about violent behaviour from a partner. Their questions follow the Duluth model of power and control (Pence and Paymar, 1986), e.g.:

1. Do you feel safer when I talk to you alone?
2. Do you believe that your partner/spouse ever hit a former spouse or lover?
3. Have you ever called, or thought of calling, the police because you feared an argument was getting out of control?
4. Does your partner/spouse treat his parents roughly?
5. Do you feel free to invite your family and friends to your home?
6. Is your partner/spouse suspicious of your every move?
7. When drinking alcohol, does your partner/spouse get rough or violent?
8. Are your children scared when your partner/spouse is angry?
9. Has your partner/spouse ever hurt or killed a pet?

We always include this list as part of our teaching pack.

However, whether or not a practitioner knows about domestic violence, decisions must always be made about whom to see, when, in what order and in which combination. We agree with Stith et al. (1998) that, if safety can be assured, there are a number of reasons for doing couples' work, such as the woman might be empowered within the therapy process, many couples are already in therapy when violence is disclosed, women will sometimes choose to stay with their partner, and the levels of risk can be assessed on a case-by-case basis and a session-by-session basis. So, for all these reasons, we believe that having a designated service or, at the very least, a clear domestic violence policy is crucial in providing a comprehensive service for men, women and children that promotes safety.

No-violence contracts and safety strategies

As we describe elsewhere in the book, we work with men and women who are violent to their partners, and with parents and grown-up children. We shall restrict this discussion to men as partners, although we use these safety strategies when working with violence in other intimate and family relationships. We do not work with men who use their violence against their partners in cool and instrumental ways, designed only to control their partner's behaviour (Jacobson and Gottman, 1998). We are careful to try to screen out men who behave without empathy, because we are not convinced that therapeutic approaches, as we currently understand and use them, can be helpful. Rather they create a context whereby such people can learn more about a partner's vulnerability and use it against her. The men with whom we work are likely to behave in hot, angry and jealous ways, out of frustration and feelings of powerlessness, despite their sense of entitlement to use violence, and their partner's felt experience of their powerfulness! In their review of the demographic research, Holtzworth-Munroe and Stuart (1994) estimate that about half of the men who behave violently towards their women partners do not behave violently in other social contexts, such as at work, in the pub, on the roads, at the gym, and so on.

The use of no-violence contracts has been discussed in the context of family and couples work by Carpenter and Treacher (1989). In our work, no-violence contracts can be written or verbal. Some of the people with whom we work are not literate. We discuss the implications of literacy for our work in Chapter 7. Either way, no-violence contracts are important cooperative agreements, and we see our task as helping to develop safety strategies, to review the effectiveness of the no-violence contract, to adapt the contract to changing family circumstances and to offer 'top-up' work to help maintain the no-violence contract in the future. It is not unusual for us to work with a man individually, whose partner has ended the relationship because of his violent behaviour towards her, with his possible future relationships in mind. Such a man would want to work for safety in future relationships, so that he can recover his self-respect, find ways of talking honestly about his past behaviour with future partners, and show himself that he can live safely and be safe around others.

On the whole, our no-violence contracts are verbal, and witnessed and agreed at our three-way review meetings. They are agreements to stop the violence. As we say above, we will not undertake family reunification or couples' therapy until safety can be shown to work. If we are working with a couple, and the man is known to have behaved violently, our initial meetings with his partner are consultative only. Her involvement as a consultant to the no-violence contract, and involvement in safety planning is crucial to the success of the contract, whether or not they continue to live together, or continue to see each other. Thus the no-violence contract is as important for a separated couple, e.g. if they should meet in the street, at friends or at the contact handover meetings with their children. We discuss this further below. When the no-violence contracts are written, it is usually because another agency requires a written contract, such as Social Services, as part of child protection proceedings, or because the perpetrator of violence understands the written word to be more binding or significant in some way, e.g. we worked with a non-residential father who had behaved violently towards his adolescent daughter. As a result, she refused to meet with him again. He wanted a written no-violence contract so that he could lodge it with a solicitor as evidence for his daughter of his commitment to try to change. He understood that this required no acknowledgement or action from her unless she wanted to read the contract letter and/or make contact with him. We understood the no-violence contract to be an important first step in him taking responsibility for his violent behaviour.

We use a mix of behavioural, cognitive and systemic problem-solving methods to help family members who have behaved violently to maintain their no-violence contracts, develop safety strategies and implement them. Each no-violence contract has an agreed safety plan. The most popular safety strategy with couples and family members is the 'time-out' strategy. In our work, violent behaviour usually occurs when people express different opinions or perceive a personal threat or felt injustice, or they are in conflict and it is difficult to reach agreement or compromise or otherwise to negotiate their differences. Time out can be called by either partner, with either a verbal or a non-verbal 'T' sign, and whoever calls it, and whenever it is called, the other must also undertake to act on it. When time out is called, both partners must agree to stop their discussion or argument, despite their feelings of entitlement to pursue a point! We advise men to leave the house and go into the garden if possible. They may walk round the block or undertake some physical activity. We ask men if they can feel themselves calming down as they walk around. Many men tell us that brisk physical activity helps reduce their feelings of muscular tension. We do not advise getting into cars or using motor cycles in this state of mind. We advise women to go to another room, where there is an outside exit. We do not advise retreat into an upstairs bedroom or bathroom without an exit. We advise women not to block the partner's exit from the room or to pursue the partner.

It is important that time out is not seen to be used as a way of avoiding important issues in their relationship and that they both have responsibilities to make their relationship work, even though the man has responsibility for his past violent behaviour. We have found that some women fear that the man is leaving for good when he leaves for 'time out', so it has been important to encourage men to find a way to say, 'I am taking time out, not leaving', and for her to acknowledge this. This can be a small mark of acknowledgement and cooperation in the heightened anxiety and arousal of the moment. Hence we see the importance of the woman partner's agreement to the use of time out as a safety strategy. After an agreed period of 'calming down', it may be possible for the couple to resume their discussion, or it may not be safe to do so. In that case, we recommend waiting until they meet with us again, or taking the discussion to a trusted third person, such as an extended family member, trusted friend, faith leader or whoever would be culturally appropriate for such a task.

In our experience, regular rehearsal of the safety plan makes its implementation in the heat of the moment more likely. We look into the future and try to predict what difficulties they think they will have in using time out and help them problem-solve alternatives. We help men to recognize anger's early warning signs (Novaco, 1975) and to develop self-management strategies in response. Many men with whom we work are tentative at first in identifying, naming and understanding their own physiological arousal responses, cognitive processes, such as self talk, and personal triggers, such as perceived provocation, injustice, transgression, and so on. We spend a lot of time uncovering and talking through examples of past harm, both from them to their partners, and from others to them when they were younger, helping men articulate and name their experiences, with a view to a more emotionally intelligent responsiveness in the future. If we can help men to find ways of holding the older generation responsible for how they were treated as children, it seems to help them develop their sense of responsibility for how they treat their partners and children. The recognition that they may have been shamed as children is an integral part of our therapeutic work with men. It is important that the men understand that our wish is not to shame them further, but to help them take responsibility for their behaviour and to put safety first, as a means of regaining their own self-respect and treating others with decency.

So, in order to plan for safety, and develop a time-out strategy, we need to understand and explain what conditions, behaviours, attitudes, and so on, make violent behaviour more likely as an interpersonal response. We work with the worst and/or last episode of violence and carefully track the escalation into physical violence in detail. We are interested in what happens, when, and by whom, and witnessed by whom, in sequence. We contextualize this episode of violent behaviour by identifying the proximal and distal risk factors. Distal risk factors may be conditions of living that cause stress and distress, such as debt, poor housing, stress and bullying at work, worries about extended family, poor social support networks, experience of childhood abuse, and so on, which may affect an individual's well-being and tolerance for frustration. Proximal risk factors may be the patterns of beliefs and rules that could be said to govern an individual's perception of choice and entitlement to respond with violence when frustrated, irritated, wanting their own way, feeling they have been treated unjustly, and so on. We pay special attention to the particular triggers for violence and their interconnection, such as a person's thoughts, feelings and awareness of physiological arousal. These feelings can be understood in the context of patriarchal entitlements, power imbalances in current relationships and lack of respect in relationships, both now and in childhood. Once the no-violence contract for physical assault has been established and seems to be holding, as reported by all concerned parties at our regular review meetings, we extend it to include other forms of psychological abuse, such as coercive and intimidatory behaviours. The pro-feminist work on violence in intimate partner relationships, carried out by the staff of the Duluth Domestic Abuse Intervention Project (Pence and Paymar, 1986), has drawn our attention to behaviours of 'emotional terrorism' that form the context for acts of violence, and that may well continue within a relationship once actual physical violence has ceased. These behaviours which serve to humiliate, shame and degrade the other may sometimes also be initiated by the recipient of violent behaviour as part of self-defence, and buttressed sometimes by a sense of entitlement as a victim of physical abuse. At this point we are then able to extend the no-violence contract to look more carefully at past issues and how they impact on the present and the hopes for the future, widening the scope and context of questioning, explanation and possible solutions.

The use of time-out strategies to support the no-violence contract is usually a short-term strategy. As the work progresses, and safety is established, both as a new entitlement and as a corroborated practice, we may move into other forms of couples' work. Now, we are more likely to develop further work on communication and negotiation skills, and help develop mutual understanding and different methods of support.

If a no-violence contract is broken, we do not keep information about repeat violence confidential. Our first response is to call a review meeting with all three (at least) participants within our minimum sufficient network triangle. Couples and family members are aware of the moral position we take around violence, our beliefs about violence and safety in relationships, and our reasons for doing this work. We always try to talk to family members about our use of social control procedures. We do not try to repeatedly shore up the no-violence contract. When doing couples' work, depending on what happened, we may well try to implement the no-violence contract one more time, with the agreement of all parties. If it is not considered safe to do so, we do not abandon people. We might refer the perpetrator back to a men's group or offer more individual work around anger management, and offer the woman individual support in liaison with Women's Aid services. It may be possible to resume couples' work at a later stage, if all participants agree and the man has shown that he can prioritize safety. Liaison between all parties is crucial in effective safety planning and in the timing of the different interventions available (Vetere and Cooper, 2001b).

CHAPTER 3

The culture of language and violence

The importance of multiple theories

In developing our ideas on working with family and intimate partner violence, and in being challenged by the complexity of thinking about the family, the family–agency relationship, including that with ourselves, and the professional network as an interlinking system, we agree with Goldner and her colleagues (Goldner et al., 1990; Goldner, 1998, 1999) that we need multiple theories to understand these many layered situations. Therapists need to link the history of emotional relationships and family developments where dilemmas and binds within those relationships intersect with violence, coercion and abuses of power. These are the relationships where expectations and patterns of dependence, independence and attachment develop (Vetere and Cooper, 2000, 2001b). We accept the premise that we as therapists are organized by and subject to the same cultural prescriptions, proscriptions and stereotypes about gender, culture and ethnicity as the family members we work alongside. Thus we find multiple theories helpful, both in grounding our practice in systemic formulation (Vetere and Dallos, 2003) and in holding ourselves ethically accountable for our practice.

In some of the systemic family therapy literature, it has been argued that couples' therapy should never be employed once domestic violence is identified (Kaufman, 1992; Rivett, 2001). Such blanket statements may lead some therapists and domestic violence practitioners simply to dismiss concerns about couples or parenting issues or even the wishes and needs of the children, and work either individually or in single gender groups. It could also be argued that therapists are well placed, when they prioritize safety and responsibility, to understand the emotional development and needs of those who perpetrate violence on others, as a prerequisite for change. Although these positions contribute to the polarization in the field, we would argue for multiple theories and approaches because of the complex nature of the issues when working with family violence.

Domestic violence takes many different forms, so it is unlikely that a single treatment modality will be maximally effective (Bograd and Mederos, 1999). Many of the treatment approaches in current use are group programmes designed for male offenders, which concurrently support the women and children. These group programmes have been subjected to the most research evaluation. The treatment aims may vary somewhat according to the theoretical orientation of the group programme, but the emphasis on protection for women and children, and on accountability for the male perpetrator, are paramount. Group programmes appear to be effective in helping some men stop their violent behaviour, but there is no one treatment approach that has been shown to suit all men (Dobash et al., 1999; Dunford, 2000; Stith et al., 2002) and some suggestion that other interventions, such as positive arrest police policies, can be as effective. In addition, a few studies have suggested that some group treatment programmes may contribute to unanticipated negative effects for some of the men and their women partners, e.g. Dutton (1986) reported that a significant proportion of women partners reported an increase in verbal abuse since their partners attended the group programme; Tolman (1990) reported that men may go home believing that their wives have little to complain about because they see themselves as less verbally abusive of women than other men in the group; or, as Gondolf (2002) reported, 10–15 per cent of women partners said that their lives had significantly worsened since their male partners began attending the group programme. Conversely, there has been less research evaluation of couples' therapy for domestic violence. In their recent review of the available research, Stith et al. (2002) conclude that domestic violence-focused therapy, with carefully screened couples, appears to be at least as effective in reducing assaultative behaviour as men's groups and individual treatment for men. Importantly, in the research reviewed, none of the couples' programmes was assessed to be more dangerous in outcome than the gender-specific treatments.

Over the past eight years, we have worked with upwards of 400 families and couples, of which about one-third have been court assessments, either within child care proceedings or in child custody/contact disputes. Within this third, about half have been risk assessments carried out within on-going therapeutic rehabilitation in the aftermath of domestic violence. A successful outcome for us is the cessation of violence, as far as we can know from our multiple sources. Thus, a successful outcome can be found in a couple separating safely, or in a previously violent father and husband sustaining safe supervised contact with the children.

We assess outcomes in a number of ways. Within our therapeutic work, we seek feedback at every couples' and family meeting, during our regular reviews with shared information from all the perspectives in our minimum sufficient network triangle, at a final evaluation meeting, and at regular follow-up and top-up meetings for at least a year. We have more control over our therapeutic work than our court work, and we have found it harder to seek information about outcomes within our court work because feedback has been patchy. Our letters and closing reports to other professional workers are always copied to our clients. We use some of the assessment instruments from the *Framework for Children in Need and their Families* (Department of Health, 2000) at different times in our work. We have very low non-attendance and drop-out rates, probably because external motivation to attend meetings with us is high, and some of the violent behaviour is already known.

As systemic thinkers, we believe that changes can take place at a number of interrelated levels:

- changes in behaviour and behavioural patterns, e.g. stopping violent actions and responses, and finding other means to understand and resolve differences;
- changes in beliefs and belief systems, such as unpicking, understanding, challenging and giving up on beliefs around unquestioned entitlement to control others' thoughts, actions and responses;
- changes in emotional patterns and attachments in intimate relationships, such as less tension, more trust and more straight talking in response to less use of coercive strategies;
- changes in relationships with wider contexts, such as family members' commitment to cooperate with professional workers and community members (Vetere and Dallos, 2003).

Thus, our systemic framework promotes change by drawing on both family systems' thinking and theories from other disciplines, integrating them in assessment, formulation, intervention and evaluation. A systemic formulation drives our approach to safety, responsibility, and therapeutic explanation and practice. Systemic formulation focuses on the problem of violence and its maintaining patterns and feedback loops, the beliefs and explanations for violent behaviour, emotional responses and attachments, and cultural and contextual factors, from the perspectives of all three participating perspectives (the family members, ourselves and our stable third, usually our referrers). Vetere and Dallos (2003) have suggested that systemic formulation is sympathetic to the practices of other disciplines because it (1) is a holistic approach, (2) makes use of working hypotheses, (3) is a multidimensional approach, (4) is a multiperspective approach (integrates a variety of theoretical positions), (5) offers a critical and reflective orientation and (6) supports an evidence-based orientation.

In our work, we are informed by ideas of pattern and process in relationships, of the intergenerational transmission of attitudes and beliefs towards violence, of intergenerational and life cycle experiences and the context of the referral (Vetere and Cooper, 2001b). Feminist-informed sociopolitical critiques of power in interpersonal relationships (Burck and Speed, 1995) provide the context for drawing on object relations ideas when thinking about intimate attachments, internalized working models of relationships and representations of self and others, and the dilemmas and binds that underpin violence in family relationships (Akister, 1998). Social learning theory helps us unpack the gendered constructions around masculinity and femininity, while paying attention to the family and social processes that acculturate children (Browne and Herbert, 1997). We weave Novaco's (1993) work in developing a cognitive–behavioural approach to anger management and arousal regulation into both our risk assessment and our risk management approaches.

Feminist linguists

We have been very influenced by the work of the feminist linguists, whose work helps us to explore: (1) how women and men might use language differently and the implications of this for therapy; (2) how beliefs come from very subtle teachings as well as the history of each family who will regard these beliefs in particular ways and with unique importance; and (3) how we can listen for words and phrases of responsibility and change within our conversations with our clients. The folk linguistics of each family is a way of understanding how ideas, beliefs and meaning get transmitted from generation to generation to both women and men (Coates, 1986; Anderson, 1988; Cooper, 1989).

We seek to understand whether and how violence is talked about at home and in relationships, e.g.

- What words do people use to talk about violent behaviour, responsibility, accountability, apology and forgiveness?
- Do they have the words to talk about violent acts and the consequences for individual family members and their relationships?
- Are there family rules that govern whether it is permissible to talk about violent behaviour?

If such talk is taboo, and there is no shared family history of discussing violent events, harm, healing and the complex consequences for relationships, the loyalties that underpin such a taboo can be strong and enduring. We worked with an extended family where the women sought comfort and refuge with one another when one of them was assaulted by her husband. The assault was not talked about with the men or, as far as we could tell, by the men. When the young wife and her husband sought our help to break these established patterns, they risked alienation from both the men and the women in the extended family. See Chapter 5 for a further description of this work.

The use of language and systemic therapy

The field of family therapy has become increasingly attentive to concepts about language and language use. As family therapists, we use language not only to communicate but also to create new meanings and connections between therapist and client. It is the means by which our clients describe themselves to us, the means by which we describe ourselves to them, and part of the way we co-evolve a dialogue with them (Cooper, 1989; Serra, 1993; Boscolo et al., 1994; Penn and Frankfurt, 1994; Andersen, 1996; Goldner, 1999). However, it is also noticeable that most theories of family life and family therapy give little attention to ideas about language use, communicative competence, gender as an influential variable in language use, and the complex meanings of everyday language and speech patterns.

As we regard violent behaviour as a strategy of social control and intimidation within intimate relationships, we are interested in the relationship between the use of language and volitional behaviour. Language is one of a number of power bases or personal resources on which family members draw in order to maintain influence (Williams and Watson, 1988). When assessing for therapeutic rehabilitation or for a court assessment, we listen carefully to how family members talk about their responsibility for violent behaviour, e.g. whether their use of words minimizes or diminishes the acts of violence (Cooper, 1989; Hearn, 1994) or the responsibility and intentionality for those acts. Paradoxically, the experience and expression of anger and violent behaviour are often described colloquially as 'losing it', not 'gaining it'. This excuse of anger makes an appeal to both impulse and biological inevitability. However, anger and aggression are different – the former does not have to lead to the latter. The potential to diffuse responsibility for violent behaviour is present in descriptions of helpless, out-of-control perpetrators. There are many unusual juxtapositions of words in everyday language that describe the opposite or minimize what is perceived, felt or intended, e.g. a father said of his adolescent daughter, after hitting her, 'she knows I love her, the silly cow, she knows I won't do it again.' He framed his entire promise to his daughter in words of love and good intentions but not in words of responsibility or accountability, nor did he show any relational or empathic understanding of her position as his daughter. It was the therapeutic work of unpicking these phrases that allowed him to consider what his daughter did need from him and most importantly what his responsibilities were as her father. Another example can be found in the use of the common linguistic tag, 'I know that doesn't

excuse my behaviour', when we offer an explanation of why we did something that has hurt or offended someone. It is as if we recognize in common parlance the tendency to fudge responsibility with explanation (Vetere and Cooper, 2001a).

The work of the feminist linguists has been helpful in thinking about the complexity of language use in our work. Language use became an important issue for feminists in the late 1960s and 1970s, because they were concerned about negative images of women and the importance of language in creating these images (Lakoff, 1975; Spender, 1980; Gilligan, 1982; Coates and Cameron, 1988). The feminist challenge to conventional thinking rested on arguments based on taken-for-granted stereotypes and distortions. The critical analysis that came out of this period undoubtedly led to many organizational and language changes and at last introduced a wider debate about gender within the family therapy literature (Cooper, 1989; Tannen, 1991; Lakoff, 2000).

Crawford (1995) warns of the danger in the assumption that 'gender is difference'. Such a definition, she maintains, involves a static, bipolar and categorical view of what constitutes gender and the language of gender that captures neither the dynamic nature of language used by both genders in differing social contexts nor the crucial point that it is the language used that helps determine the social organization. Systemic therapists have been uneasy with the discourse of difference because there is a danger that a polarized entity can support existing institutions and reproduce existing power relations. By understanding the active nature of language, systems therapists and theoreticians of gender have moved forward out of this dichotomy to adopt positions allowing methodological plurality. However, it is important that this plurality encompass a moral, ethical and political view, and knowledge of issues such as gendered language and its effects and meanings. For the clinician trying to understand the meanings and effects of violent behaviour, these different levels of meaning can be the turning point of our observations and can add a new level of meaning to the relationship patterns that we observe (Cooper, 1989), e.g. oppressive talk reinforces and recreates oppression in human relationships and the words available to talk about violence will most probably reflect the family rules about whether it is even permissible to talk about violence, for men, women or children.

In a society where men and women are considered to be different, language not unexpectedly both reflects and maintains these differences (Spender, 1980). We acquire language and communicative competence through a learning process that is shaped by the values of our culture and particular forms of gender socialization about violence and violent behaviour, filtered through family relationships. Social order can be said to be reproduced and partly maintained through language use, in different social institutions, including the family, so it is interesting to consider how these language patterns, linguistic rules and social expectations come to be believed and accommodated in particular ways by men and women, including ourselves as therapists (Anderson, 1988; Cooper, 1989; Lakoff, 2000).

Goldner and colleagues (Goldner et al., 1990; Goldner, 1998, 1999) have identified four ways in which the above ideas are of particular importance when thinking about problematic complementarities in relationships where one partner is violent to the other:

1. in talking with both partners about developing a commitment to transcend rigid categories of gender difference, which helps make it possible for them to begin to tolerate their disowned similarities, such as men acknowledging their sensitivities and feelings, and women acknowledging their competence;
2. to encourage the idea that change in behaviour, beliefs and relationships is possible;
3. for a woman, to reclaim a sense of independent subjectivity and to establish or re-establish her capacity for independent agency;
4. for a man to accept responsibility for his behaviour and his dependency needs, and to be able to empathize with his partner's subjective experiences.

In our work we explore and unpack the complex weave of power and control, stereotypical and atypical gender experiences and expectations, and the beliefs and assumptions that are implicit in our individual language use. Holmes (1992) suggests that women and men talk about the social world in different ways, while also talking in ways that illustrate solidarity and connection. Understanding the influences of stereotypical and atypical gendered speech patterns, while at the same time challenging the meaning of these stereotypical patterns and exploring the potential for change latent in the atypical patterns, allows us to listen in a different way to women and to men, so that they maximize their potential for change, even though some social and family rules appear to oppose change.

Although the experience of learning gendered language can be seen as contributing to the development of our identity, it is not easy to remember how or when it has been learned. It is complicated to think back and unpack what our families' beliefs were about being a boy or girl, man or woman, father or mother; or to remember the taboos about what could or could not be talked about; or the gendered language rules about social behaviour like 'women should not shout' (language about power and its uses) or 'real men do not cry' (language about emotion). These cultural and family rules are all part of the taken for grantedness of everyday life; they are handed down from one generation to the next and form the folk linguistics of everyday life. Intergenerational transmission of meanings and beliefs is often grudgingly acknowledged as being unchangeable (Coates, 1986; Coates and Cameron, 1988; Cooper, 1989).

In talking about violent behaviour in therapy and assessment, the descriptions and explanations of the perpetrator of violence and the descriptions and explanations of the victim of violence are both valid. However, we are listening in detail for language that promotes and accepts responsibility for violent behaviour from the perpetrator and language that acknowledges the right of safety and a sense of agency on the part of the victim. Combination talk that can include responsibility and exclude responsibility is often complicated (Hearn, 1994). This combination talk slips and slides between responsibility and the potential for change, on the one hand, and then slides back into entitlement on the other. To the listener, it can often sound like a muddle, especially if delivered fast and with conviction. Therefore it needs specially honed listening skills and a request to 'slow down so I can listen and understand'. Individual phrases, such as 'I only pushed her' or 'I just shoved her' or 'She got in the way of my fist' permit minimization if they pass by the therapist without comment or challenge. We would seek to deconstruct these minimizations, asking about context, intentionality and safety. We hear men talking about holding women responsible for provoking them: 'She knew when she said that she was going to get hit' or 'She was asking for it!' It is as if the men hold women responsible for their arousal regulation and anger control.

When they project blame outwards, they often do so with a sense of entitlement and with fluency. Alongside this, we sometimes hear women say that they deserved to get hit. 'I deserved a good hiding', a young woman told us when she described how she had 'deliberately provoked' her male partner by flirting with other men at a party. When we hear women taking the blame for their male partner's violent behaviour towards them, we deconstruct these comments, and the underlying beliefs, in the same way we would statements that minimize responsibility for aggressive behaviour. We notice patterns in some opposite-sex couple relationships whereby the man will diminish his responsibility for his actions, and the woman will tolerate that description. Similarly, the woman may diminish her sense of competence in the way she describes herself, and he will support that description and tolerate her putting herself down. In our reading of the literature on working therapeutically with domestic violence, we note that much of the writing consistently describes men as 'batterers', rather than as men, partners and/or fathers who beat or assault their women partners. We find this practice, of describing men only by their violent actions, as unhelpful as always describing their women partners as 'victims'. The risk for us is that people come to be seen in one-dimensional ways and, given the

arguments around the active nature of language use in shaping our per-
ceptions, this may well contribute to beliefs that men cannot change.

As our therapeutic dialogue does not necessarily follow stereotypical
patterns of linguistic interaction, it is also important to recognize that the
way a question is constructed, and the beliefs and meanings that it con-
tains, determine in part the answer that can be given (Coates, 1986;
Anderson and Goolishian, 1988; Cooper, 1989). Therefore when talking
about violent behaviour, we make it clear that we regard the speaker and
listener as equally important. Even if one of the couple is shy and fearful,
we introduce the idea of equity in our work and do our best to maintain
that focus. So, in listening and talking about violent behaviour, the
descriptions and explanations of both the victim and the perpetrator are
valid. However, we also keep in mind the finding that violent behaviour
alters the meaning of non-violent communications, including non-verbal
communications, and remember that 'intonation always lies at the border
of the verbal and non-verbal, the said and the unsaid' (Volosinov, 1972).

We regard tone and intentionality as part of the intimidatory process.
These issues are often delicate and difficult to untangle, but are important
because, if the perpetrator stops physically violent behaviour but continues to intimidate, through attitude, tone, facial expression, physical
posture and use of language, then only partial change has been achieved
(Vetere and Cooper, 2001b). In understanding change and the ability to
change, with regard to safety, it is particularly useful to consider speaker
innovation. From a linguistic point of view, Coates and Cameron (1988,
p. 21) write about speaker innovation in the following way:

> Language does not, however, exist apart from language users; speech does
> not exist independently of speakers. So we need to make a distinction
> between linguistic change, which is in the language system, and speaker
> innovation, which describes the role played by speakers in initiating linguis-
> tic change. The study of linguistic change has a long history, but our
> understanding of the role played by individual speakers is still in its infancy.

In developing our methodology we regard ideas about language change
and speaker innovation to be relevant when working with the constraints
and opportunities of domestic violence. The therapist by listening closely
can encourage and notice acts of speaker innovation that can change the
beliefs, behaviours and meanings influencing both speakers and listeners,
and such acknowledgement can add richness to the therapeutic
encounter. Alongside our interest in language use, we have taken into
account an understanding of the relationship between the spoken word
and written text. This has formed part of our methodology. At Reading
Safer Families we regard both writing and speaking as expressive modes
that together set up an iterative process, each influencing the other.

Written and spoken words

In developing our methodology we were interested in the fact that, because we both work in the room as part of a reflecting process, we are simultaneously spectator and participant in both modes of writing and speaking (Ong, 1982; Penn and Frankfurt, 1994). The therapeutic process demands that we reflect upon the difference between written texts and spoken language and the processes involved. Our therapy notes are written during the meeting and are available to our clients. They form the basis of any report and we encourage our clients to contribute to the notes if they wish. Therefore, when we offer the family the opportunity of being actively involved in recording the session, it serves to extend the scope of collaboration and co-construction by bringing into the therapy itself a recording activity that is usually done by the therapist alone outside the session.

Many of the clients we meet in our project are non-literate, so we ask routinely about their reading and writing skills, who helps them and whom they can trust to read to them. This is especially pertinent when considering court reports. Perhaps it is with these clients who do not take writing for granted that the written word and our attempts to understand their struggle with it are most important. The complexity of this issue for a couple when the man is non-literate and the woman literate was illustrated for us when we understood the danger she was in whenever reading was required, e.g. the couple had a disagreement about the right way to get to our office and, when he asked his partner to read the map, she refused. His anger in response was almost uncontainable, in the car, in our waiting room and in our office, during our meeting. We met this couple, separately and together, as part of a court assessment. The trigger of literacy did not diminish.

The constraint of the written word is that it comes to be seen as privileged and the most accurate record. In some of our court assessment work, we receive bundles of reports and documents that may date back over many years. We read these documents carefully, as we sometimes notice that ideas raised hypothetically in some earlier documents get repeated in later documents as statements. We pay attention to the wider professional and legal system, and describe our use of the spoken word and written text in our court reports. This both informs the court and allows us to speak to our reflective process if we are called to give evidence as expert witnesses. In our court reports, for example, we write the following:

> Jan Cooper has been the lead interviewer during the assessment meetings and Dr Arlene Vetere has been the in-room consultant, and took notes during the meetings. Our internal consultation process enables us to develop

our ideas both in the room and between assessment meetings in discussion
and to be fed back into the interview process in subsequent meetings.

A useful reflective question for us as therapists to ask at the end of a
reporting process is: 'What will happen if this account is never challenged
by the family?'

To end this chapter on a self-reflective note, we include the work of
Lamb (1991). Her thinking helps us question and challenge our own ways
of writing and describing people, their relationships, acts and events. She
surveyed academic journal research reports on men's violence to known
women, and identified problems in the academic writing that contributed
to further minimization of the problem of men's violence. Such writing
strategies included the following:

• diffusion of responsibility, such as using collective terms like 'domestic
  violence' or 'spouse abuse' that hide the gender of the perpetrator of
  violence, or the victim of violence;
• the use of the passive voice in writing, such as describing acts without
  agents;
• nominalization, such as using terms like 'the violence', 'the abuse';
• naming victims without agents, such as referring to the woman as
  'battered' without naming the man or woman who did the 'battering';
• gender obfuscation, such as using terms like 'the victim' or 'the
  perpetrator'.

Such a list helps us in thinking about where we can use full phrases,
such as 'a man behaving aggressively towards his woman partner', rather
than a term like 'domestic violence', or 'batterer', in such a way that this
text does not become cumbersome for the reader, yet the reader sees the
golden thread of 'subjects, verbs and objects', grammatically speaking!

CHAPTER 4

Reflection and collaboration in the therapeutic process

Developing a reflecting process

When we decided to create a therapeutic and assessment service that acknowledged the impact of the effects of domestic violence at the point of referral, we considered what would be the most positive model of therapy. We debated whether we should use a one-way screen, with one of us sitting behind it in a consultative role, as might be expected within a systemically oriented service. We doubted the wisdom of this choice, however, because this client group have often been through a lengthy legal process and been subject to intense scrutiny by professional staff. Thus, a screen-and-team model seemed too intrusive, too watchful and not sufficiently collaborative for this kind of work. Therefore, we decided to work together in the therapy room and combine 'live' supervision and the 'reflecting process'. It is the synthesis of these two roles that enables us to develop our ideas with our clients both in the room and between sessions, and to provide feedback into the interview process in subsequent meetings. One of us (AV) came to a similar conclusion when setting up a systemic couples and family therapy service, at the same time, in the local community alcohol service.

The combination of 'live' supervision and reflecting processes is a development of Bateson's original idea: 'the method of double or multiple comparison' (Bateson, 1979, p. 227). Using the example of a pair of binoculars, Bateson showed how a comparison from more than one perspective can give an extra dimension to what is observed. In his particular example, it was the case of depth. Bateson (1979, p. 91) speaks of the synthesis of descriptions in the following way:

> Interesting phenomena occur when two or more rhythmic patterns are combined, and those phenomena illustrate very aptly the enrichment of information that occurs when one description is combined with another.

This influential 'double description', as it became known in systemic therapy, was further developed by Andersen (1987), who described the work of his team in north Norway where they experimented using the team behind the screen to comment in front of the family. This was a most important article and built on earlier attempts to make the thinking of the team or in-room consultant readily available to all participants in the therapy process for comment and further reflection. Since that time there has been a diverse and creative expansion in the use of the reflecting process and reflecting teamwork. These ideas encouraged more transparency in systemic methods of working which finds a good fit with post-modernist and social constructionist approaches to therapy. Such a fit promotes the acknowledgement of difference and similarity at all levels of working, within individuals, between individuals, between subgroups, and between larger community and professional groups. This frame further expands the work of the Milan group on the development of meaning as a vehicle for change, and links with group analytic approaches, in that the reflecting comments can offer a different, kinder mirror to family groups than the harsher or more critical mirror that they might, at times, hold up to each other.

Contextually our therapeutic work builds a bridge for interpretation between the written documents and the spoken word, but it also places us in the position of authority, power and accountability for our work. These are poignant areas of our work, moving as they do between experiences and accounts of failure, shame and responsibility. It is in these areas that we understand whether our clients can begin to cooperate with yet another set of professionals and how their attitude to the work between us develops.

In developing our methodology we decided to divide the work equally between the role of lead therapist and in-room consultant, with the lead therapist doing most of the talking and the in-room consultant taking notes and reflecting on the process. We see families, in turn, changing our roles with each new referral. The note-taking actively incorporated the written word alongside the spoken word. In this way, our particular weave of therapeutic work and reflective peer consultation, in action, formed the core methodology for our work. It has allowed us to bring an appreciation and respect for difference, provided opportunities to consider multiple perspectives, both those present in the room and those without the room, and required a commitment to safety in a coherent way for all of us. It also encourages a culture of responsibility where we can all strive for clarity, and which in turn offers our clients an opportunity to comment on our ability to understand them or not, and for them to reflect actively on our ideas and our practice.

When working with violence in the family, both therapeutically and for assessment purposes, we think this methodology offers a number of advantages for risk management (Vetere and Cooper, 2003):

* It allows us to build trust and openness with our clients, referrers and others.
* We can be clear about our own moral position around the use of violence in family and other intimate relationships.
* We can comment on the therapeutic and assessment process as it unfolds.
* We can harness the different perspectives in the room, and call up other helpful perspectives from those not present, in combination.
* We use the same reflecting process when we talk to other professionals at review meetings.
* It promotes a co-evolving process in which everyone has a responsible part to play.

Our definition of reflecting has the same meaning as the French word 'reflexion': something heard is taken in and thought over, and the thought is given back (Andersen, 1987; Friedman, 1995). In our work we include our clients in our theoretical thinking and talk over our developing ideas with them, explaining why we think as we do, and incorporating their ideas and feedback into our further thinking. Generally speaking, we describe the reflecting process and the double description to them in the following way:

> . . . most often in life we are in conversation with each other. Very seldom do we have an opportunity to discuss something that really matters to us and then listen to two other people discussing those issues from our point of view – and then, even more crucially, have the chance to say what we think about what we've just heard.

When we conduct assessments we specifically ask clients to engage in conversation with us because experience has taught us that, particularly in court assessments, clients can be unsure about the process in which they are engaged. They may be very anxious, defensive and/or protective of others about the implications of what they say or feel unable to say. Issues about informed consent can be raised at every meeting if necessary, if it seems helpful. For many experiences in life, we need to take part before we can know to what we are consenting! So, in understanding this particular development of the reflecting process, it is important to acknowledge the diversity of the two roles of lead therapist and in-room consultant, and how we think they blend together. In the first instance it is necessary that overall responsibility for the session is held equally and that both of us feel accountable to the client(s) and the referrer(s) (Smith and Kingston, 1980). We think it is crucial that systemic therapists and trainees pay equal attention to the importance of developing both these sets of skills. We shall consider these roles from the point of view of the in-room consultant and then from that of the lead therapist.

The reflecting process from the point of view of the in-room consultant

The role of the in-room consultant is essentially a listening one. It allows time to reflect, and some emotional distance and space can be put in between the action in the room and the translation into written words, and a potential reader whose expectations and intentions may be different or entirely unknown (Ong, 1982). The active stillness of this role offers a range of creativity and containment. There is an intellectual rigour that goes with the in-room consultant's task and, although in the main it is a silent task, the in-room consultant can be called on at any time to contribute and it is a matter of importance to make those interventions brief and constructive. When the in-room consultant speaks, it is from a position of some psychological distance that may help people listen, reflect and respond to interventions in a way that may be new to them, especially when they may be feeling vulnerable and defensive. However, the psychological distance, which is possible because the in-room consultant is not actively engaged in developing the therapeutic alliances in the same way as the lead therapist, does not mean that they are emotionally uninvolved in the work, or somehow not connected to the other participants in the room. In our experience, the role of in-room consultant is the place where you are most likely to be touched by the emotions that are hidden by the words. Sometimes it is possible to introduce this tentative understanding but at the same time the moment can be elusive, or may better be saved for later discussion.

It is an interesting dilemma for the in-room consultant to ponder about the extent to which writing the words from the discussions makes the ideas seem more certain. This in turn means that the in-room consultant should be aware of potential beliefs about the power of the written word in relation to the power of the spoken word and what this means for the others in the room. It is also important for the in-room consultant to develop a style that does not intrude into the therapeutic alliance, but recognizes that, as a potential and actual stable third in the room, all the contributions need to be even-handed. This role has the potential to be profoundly systemic in its attention to feedback and processes of reciprocity.

There are a number of opportunities for the in-room consultant to make interventions without interrupting the flow of the lead therapist–client interactions. Clearly, the active listening role of the in-room consultant carries a responsibility to monitor communicative posture and other non-verbal responses at all times in the therapy; this can be seen as part of the continuous supportive process around the therapy. These interventions have the potential to be continuous or particular, and mainly non-verbal or verbal communications, e.g. the in-room consultant can:

- support what is going well
- challenge what is being said and done while promoting and protecting the therapeutic/assessment alliance, particularly at times of emotional intensity
- confirm and validate actions, intentions and beliefs
- acknowledge loss or sadness (maybe from descriptions in court papers and other documents)
- show curiosity or seek clarification
- introduce new ideas or develop existing points of view, perhaps in a less challenging way at times of stress
- remind and/or reaffirm ideas about risk and responsibility.

As with most therapeutic endeavours, there are also a few cautionary notes that we keep in mind, e.g. do not intervene:

- at a time of heightened physiological/emotional arousal
- at a time of considerable defensiveness
- at a time of reaction to past scrutiny
- at a point where it might risk symmetrical interaction
- at a time when it could be overwhelming for family members or the perpetrator of violent behaviour.

It is important for the two therapists, in their respective roles, to reflect and discuss regularly what does not fit or causes dissonance, as well as the pieces of work that feel more complete and successful. We find that paying attention to differences of opinion between us is most productive. We amplify those differences, in order both to understand them and to help protect against the development of a mutuality that is too comfortable, which is a risk in any well-established working partnership.

The reflecting process from the point of view of the lead therapist

The lead therapist has the main spoken therapeutic task. The lead therapist introduces the way we work and explains the policy of no confidentiality. Initially it is the responsibility of the lead therapist actively to promote safety and it is the lead therapist who will establish the no-violence contract, supported by the in-room consultant. The lead therapist is also responsible for giving feedback about what relevant documents we have read, what our instructions are if it is a court report and to whom we have talked before meeting them, e.g. the referrer. We tell people if we have worked with other professionals involved with them and their family before, e.g. their social worker or health visitor, so they know whether we already have a working relationship with that person. The lead therapist is also the person who manages the interactive process where everyone can speak and be listened to.

For many of our families, the equality of opportunity to speak and the expectation that we want to hear from everyone in the room are quite revolutionary. The lead therapist will also invite the in-room consultant to speak or create an opportunity for her to comment if she wishes. The lead therapist can turn to the in-room consultant if puzzled, stuck for words or unsure about what direction to take or what issue to prioritize. This is not to suggest incompetence on the part of the lead therapist, but rather shows how a collaborative environment can be created even when people are required to come to us, by the courts, say. Although we hold overall responsibility for the direction and management of the work, there are many moments when bringing our thinking into the room, with clients 'listening in' and commenting further, micro-manages the work in a shared way. Thus, the ability to create a well-informed, rigorous and supportive working relationship is not only important for the lead therapist–in-room consultant model, but also crucial to the quality of the service offered to the client.

The review process

We integrate our ideas about the reflecting process into the review process. Our working definition of a review could be described as follows:

> . . . a review is a discussion linking together the therapy sessions, the family members' perceptions of their own progress, the family's expectations of other professional agencies and their staff, the agencies' perceptions of the family member's progress and the agencies' further expectations from the family.

In assessment and therapeutic work, we suggest a review about every four to six weeks, or four to six meetings, depending on the risk assessment and the risk management plan. However, there has to be an authenticity and a systemic understanding about the reason for the punctuation, so that it can be a somewhat fluid process by negotiation. In our experience the referrer will most often want evidence of change in the individual or family. Our reflecting process means that we can talk about the process of change from the family's point of view, from our point of view and from the professional system's point of view, by integrating our views and observations about change and the process of our relationship with the referrer and with the family members.

Importantly, this regular reviewing process can provide an antidote for 'nothing is happening', such as 'network freeze', or the 'wait for the next crisis' approach sometimes found in professional systems (Hardwick, 1994). This helps prevent the minimization or magnification of issues by either the family or the professional system, and it can provide a public arena for cooperation and collaboration that we believe contributes to the development of responsibility. In these ways we can harness the therapeutic potential of multiple observers and multiple perspectives as we continue to develop our ideas in conversation with each other in front of the family and including the referrers.

Our decision to work together in the room and our reflecting process also allows us to be alert to many of the difficulties of this type of work. Michelle Bograd writes in Bograd and Mederos (1999, p. 293):

> It is arguable that, regardless of treatment modality, minimising risk and optimising safety are central. In many cases, the presence and impact of domestic violence are not visible. The man's violence may also create distortions in the internal experience of each person and within their relationship that militates against acknowledgement of his abuse for both partners and slants the couple's public discourse toward denial and minimisation.

We would agree in essence with Bograd and Mederos. We have both experienced accounts of abusive behaviour that have been so minimized and delivered in tones of such affection and without challenge that at first the descriptions appear to be part of a safe relationship. Working in a partnership has allowed us to think about and experience these challenges. We have often been struck by the different emotional responses that we have in our different roles of lead therapist or in-room consultant. We use this diversity between us and magnify it to try to understand the process. Importantly, it also prevents us developing a 'folie a deux' and counteracts any habit we might develop of thinking and responding in predictable ways. Similarly, if the therapist and family members seem to be dealing with too much information, and are possibly emotionally overwhelmed in that moment, the in-room consultant can comment on this in a way that creates a reflective space, and allows people to decide the issues that should be given priority.

There is, and always should be, tension between the constraints and benefits of a reflecting process. We would describe these tensions in the following ways:

• It is important to make fine distinctions about when to interrupt or not, i.e. avoid intervention during the development of a theme, or a specific line of enquiry leading to responsibility and/or accountability.

- Be alert to the darker forces of envy, rivalry and competition because, then, the process is no longer useful to the family or the therapists.
- The in-room consultant/note-taker may have a very good idea, but if it is not an appropriate time to intervene, write it down (the brilliance of the idea can be explained later!).
- It is easier in the room, than from behind the screen, to be aware of timing about when to interrupt, because you are part of the emotional atmosphere in the room.
- Over time you can develop a sympathetic relationship to each other's work.
- Keep reflections simple, tentative and short, and in the context of accountability to the client and other professional workers.

In our opinion the overall reflecting process offers a variety of positive opportunities in the context of working with violence in the family, e.g. it is easy for us to develop a smooth process by asking each other's opinions or ideas and in this way we can reflect on a wide range of issues that affect family life, such as:

- generational issues
- children's development and children's views about the problem
- the family history
- promoting family success
- validation of both members of a couple and other family relationships
- comments about and understanding of the legal frame and how that impinges on family life
- asking about other family members, e.g. the views of children who may be in the care system or grandparents' views, as we can bring their presence and some of their views into the room.

Bruner (1986) says that 'there are always feelings and lived experience not fully encompassed by the dominant story.' In our project most of our referrals are described in a problem-saturated way and when we meet the clients their personal stories are nearly always blaming, of themselves and others, and accusatory. This can predict their inability to change. Our two voices are important in creating an opportunity where the clients can be both encouraged and held responsible, both to ensure future safety and for past violent behaviour. It is also where other aspects of their lived experience can contradict or be held alongside these negative narratives that are often so dominant and compelling. We have understood these processes by paying particular attention to how people live under scrutiny and 'in the goldfish bowl'. We cannot change the history but we have empowered families to feel that we have understood this important and often highly charged experience.

An example of our attention to process and our commitment to seek external consultation is exemplified by an assessment case referred by the court. The children were temporarily in the care system but living with a paternal aunt. The father was white British and the mother was from a west African country. The mother was learning English as a second language. We did not need an interpreter, but it was her accent that was difficult for us to understand and we were concerned that we were not well informed about her cultural heritage. We wrote to the court informing them that we would arrange a consultation with a specialist cultural family therapist. In addition, in conjunction with the mother's solicitor, and with our help, a psychiatrist was found who spoke the dialect of her own language. The court agreed to pay for the consultation and so an important local legal precedent was achieved.

The opportunities and constraints that this methodology produces are all part of a therapeutic style that evolves over time and influences our process. Our gender and our differing professional histories influence and subjectively construct that which we are observing and describing. For many men, sitting in the room with three women, two therapists and his partner, for example, can be intimidating. It is important to be able to use ourselves and our ability to comment on that process creatively and constructively. We might ask the man what other men would say; we might try to put ourselves in the shoes of a man, so to speak; while acknowledging our limitations, we might talk about other men with whom we have worked, and their views, dilemmas and choices; and we seek external consultation from men. We ask our clients questions in role and we find that this is helpful in understanding the development of personal and parental agency around problem-solving in the aftermath of violence. Importantly, such questions form part of our approach to risk management. Much of our thinking about role has stemmed from the particular fact that men are most often seen within the legal frame as perpetrators of violence to their family members but seldom as fathers. On the other hand, if they are seen as partners they are also simultaneously seen as perpetrators. This makes our systemic curiosity about their lives an opportunity to challenge and expand this dominant discourse while still expecting accountability and responsibility. In our experience within the professional system, men who are described as violent seldom get an opportunity to talk about themselves in a way that includes their experiences and identities as fathers.

Being able to establish conversations about overlapping identities, such as father, husband, brother, nephew, uncle, and so on, allows men to develop a sense of being a subject, not an object (Cooper, 1992). Fergal Keane (1996), a BBC foreign correspondent, gives a poignant account of intergenerational connection. He writes a letter to his newborn son

Daniel, as a first-time father, and reflects on the emotions that enable him to redefine his lost relationship with his own father. His father had previously died after being isolated from his family following years of alcoholism.

> Yet now Daniel, I must tell you that when you let out your first powerful cry in the delivery room of the Adventist Hospital and I became a father, I thought of your grandfather and foolish though it may seem, hoped that in some way he could hear across the infinity between the living and the dead, your proud statement of arrival. For if he could hear, he would recognise the distinct voice of family, the sound of hope and new beginnings that you and all your innocence and freshness have brought into the world.
>
> Keane (1996, p. 129)

Thus, the birth of his son instantly created the development of a new role that allowed his previous relationship with his father to become altered and he allowed it to become an opportunity for reflection. We have often observed how talking in role reduces defensiveness and allows the speaker more freedom.

Some of the questions that we ask fathers in role include:

* As a father, what do you want your son/daughter to learn about how men and women get on?
* As a father what will you advise your daughter to keep herself safe?
* As a father how will you hold yourself responsible to your children for your violence towards them?
* As a father how will you talk to them about these incidents when they are older?
* In your family who would be most able to discuss difficult issues with you?

In a similar way we ask mothers:

* As a mother how will you teach your daughter to recognize and want respect in a relationship?
* As a mother how do you see your relationship developing with your son/daughter over the next few years?
* When you look to the future how do you think your daughter/son will see your actions now?

Using parental questions in role allows the couple to tell us about their own sense of agency for problem-solving around their own co-parenting relationship and their relationship with their children. It also allows us to continue to assess for safety.

Case example: four women working together in a reflecting process

The following case illustrates how we slowly came to understand a complex pattern of intergenerational relationships and how we actively used our reflecting partnership as an intervention. Ms Bray was a young white British woman and mother of two girls aged 7 and 5 years. She and her children were referred by Social Services with the children's social worker as the stable third. Ms Bray was separated from the father of her children and in a new partnership that we understood was violent only after meeting with Ms Bray's mother. Ms Bray's children had been placed in the care system for the last 6 months by Social Services and there was a plan that they should be returned to her care. Ms Bray had struggled against an alcohol and drug abuse problem for some time and it was clear that she had worked very hard to get her daughters returned to her care. Shortly after we met Ms Bray, she asked if her mother could come to meet us. Mrs Down, the mother of Ms Bray, came because she was worried about her daughter's present relationship with a partner who was violent to her.

A very close relationship between mother and daughter had been forged over the years, particularly in response to Mr Down (partner of Mrs Down and father of Ms Bray) who had been consistently violent to Mrs Down and their children for many years. At the time we saw them, Ms Bray and her other adult siblings still did not leave Mrs Down alone in the flat with their father Mr Down. They managed an informal 'unspoken' rota that had existed for years. We also learnt that Mrs Down's youngest son wanted to leave home at this time to join the army and this helped us see some of the importance of protection in this family and the complexity of 'why now' in seeking outside help. In the sessions with the mother and the daughter, there was a good deal of energetic accusation and counter-accusation between them. It was some time before we understood that the two-generational pattern of accusation between daughter and mother, which was profoundly blaming, constantly justified the status quo, and diluted both of their efforts to be helpful to each other. The paradox was that Ms Bray blamed her mother for not leaving her father, whereas Mrs Down blamed her daughter for not leaving her partner. Together, in defence of their inability to leave either partner and in defence of themselves, they invalidated and minimized both the support and the abuse they received. In addition, they constantly justified their own actions by being critical and blaming of the other. This was the status quo row that had been maintained for years: Ms Bray would say to her mother: 'Don't mention violence to me, YOU would not leave Dad, look what YOU did and look what you put me through.' Mrs Down would say to her daughter: 'Don't mention violence to me, YOU won't leave your partner, look what YOU have done to your children and look what you are still putting me through and you should know better from what happened to me!'

Both mother and daughter, from both their points of view, also blamed each other for believing their partners, who regularly apologized and swore to each of them that they would not behave violently towards them again. Both of them as mothers reassured their children of their father's promise and their belief that violent behaviour would not happen again. Of course it did happen again and the children lost respect for their mothers (both generations), became even more cynical about their fathers, and developed their hypervigilant watch for their mother's safety. In the case of Mrs Down's adult children, this meant they still could not leave her in the family flat with her husband. Both mother and daughter consistently supported each other when they had been attacked and, in the immediate aftermath, both promised each other that they would leave their partner(s). Consequently, their decision to stay would disappoint and irritate the other.

For some time we diligently commented on the process, sensitively explored the options and positively commended them for their actions, but it had no effect. The opportunity of us being four women working together allowed us to make an intervention by taking their roles and replaying their parts as feedback to them in our reflecting process, for them to comment on our understanding. We could talk not only about the central dilemma of maintaining the status quo, which seemed so dangerous, but also about Ms Bray's passion for her partner as a young woman, and Mrs Down's guilt as an older woman, and her own anxiety about her daughter's potentially and actually violent behaviour for which she felt personally responsible. Initially they very quickly minimized our efforts and were dismissive of our attempts at role enactment, but we persisted and gradually it allowed them to begin to find their voice together and to develop their individual voices. By learning to trust us they were also finding themselves trustworthy in therapy and were able to progress. They could encourage each other to consider change and initiate change without it feeling too disloyal to either family or to either man. This piece of work created a new understanding of power and control. Understanding the paradox helped the women challenge the gendered intergenerational transmission of meanings and beliefs that they had maintained by such energetic helplessness!

CHAPTER 5

Children as victims, witnesses and survivors

When we started the Reading Safer Families project over eight years ago, we did not anticipate how little professional writing there would be on working therapeutically with children who witness domestic violence. There is a substantial literature on the effects on children of living in households where violent behaviour is used by their fathers against their mothers (Peled et al., 1995; Browne and Herbert, 1997). These effects may be more complicated when children are living in stepfamilies. However, there is less research specifically devoted to exploring these effects within a wider variety of family forms than the birth father–birth mother model of family living. Notwithstanding, there is much in these writings to help clinicians and other community practitioners, who meet children living in a variety of household arrangements, to identify some of the more common effects of domestic violence on children as they grow. Yet, in spite of this literature, we think it is still not easy for practitioners to identify reliably the short- and long-term effects of domestic violence on children. We take this view because children are often brought to our attention, via concerned professionals and parents/carers, who may be more oriented towards a diagnostic approach, or simply focused on the behaviours of concern, such as specific learning difficulties, social anxiety, depression, challenging behaviour, and so on, and not realizing that they indicate that the child could also be living within an abusive context.

Thus we write this chapter with a twofold purpose: to help throw light on the short- and long-term effects on children and the systemic consequences for the households who have responsibility for the welfare of children and to share our experiences of working with children troubled by their repeated exposure to violent behaviour at home. However, we need to acknowledge that we live in a culture that is strongly oriented towards violence, both institutionalized violence as in war and civil conflict, and in everyday media, such as violent films, videos, video games, music and toys. It has been argued that young men, in particular, are exposed to messages about masculinity and ways of 'proving' their manhood that involve risk, danger and harm to themselves and others (Miedzian, 1995). Conversely, how are young girls to make sense of these discourses around masculinity, and how are their aspirations to be women affected by ambivalent messages within our culture about the role of violence in our lives? We would suggest that families and household members filter the wider cultural messages to children, and provide the psychological and relational context in which violent behaviour, both inside and outside the home, is understood and given meaning.

If we argue that all boys and girls, men and women are exposed within their subcultural and wider cultural groupings to similar messages about what it is to be male and what it is to be female, we need to explain why not all boys grow into men who act with violence against women, and why not all girls grow into women who cannot say 'no'. We see these different explanations most clearly in our practice when talking intergenerationally with family members, thinking across the generations about what cultural messages may have been absorbed and filtered within the family, and what generational differences may currently divide and concern family members at the time they meet with us. We often use genograms to help trace the patterns of violent behaviour, and the beliefs and rules for behaviour that may be said to underpin these patterns, when working with adolescents, with adolescents and their family members and with 'grown-up' children and their families of origin. Genograms can illustrate the culture of violent behaviour within an extended family group and facilitate discussion of the intergenerational effects of violence.

For example, a family with whom we worked illustrates family rules about speech patterns and handing down beliefs and assumptions about behaviour over the generations. It also illustrates the courage that it takes to want change. In this particular family there was a dominant view that 'we take care of our own'. Paradoxically this view did not recognize that there were two parallel gendered stories, neither of which took into account any responsibility or understanding of the lived experiences of three generations. In sociopolitical terms the belief that 'we take care of our own' was born out of privilege, on the one hand, and family secrecy, on the other. The Limb family consisted of grandparents, their two adult daughters and one adult son. These adult children were married and the two daughters had children. Historically, the grandfather had been violent to his wife, and this violence had been witnessed by the children. The two daughters had married men who were violent towards them, and their son was violent towards his wife. It was the son's wife who went to her GP and came with her husband to see us. There seemed to be a family assumption that the men did not talk and did not need to talk about their violence towards their wives. When the women were hurt, they would go to their mother, or mother-in-law, who would look after them. The women talked about their behaviour only in terms of how it provoked the men, or in terms of closeness, support and understanding of each other. In seeking change, the young couple had to grapple with breaking the family secret, their linguistic taboo, criticism and confrontation, and, in the case of the young woman, the loss of close female company that in the past has been so supportive and important to her (Vetere and Cooper, 2001b). In the short term this young couple and their children became estranged from their family of origin, but in the long term they were influential members of the family who dared to have a different point of view about safety for themselves and their children.

Alongside our concern with the impact of westernized cultural practices on the young people with whom we work is the issue of working with cultural diversity and difference. We have written earlier in the book about the importance of being clear with clients, of any nationality or ethnicity, about the legal framework within which we live and practice, e.g. we meet men, born both within and outside the UK, who believe that it is their entitlement if not their right to beat their wives/partners for 'displeasing' them. Our approach rests firmly within the legal framework, within which we explain that their behaviour is a criminal act, despite their beliefs. Equally, their children will have been watching and learning as a result, and we think it is important that the children too are helped to realize that violent behaviour is against the law, and why. We believe that this can be done in ways that do not undermine parental or personal authority, and can fit within our various cultural and class nuances.

We practise in an area of the UK that has a relatively high proportion of diverse national and ethnic groupings, and which more recently has seen an influx of people seeking asylum. We have met with children from a range of white western groupings, such as UK nationals, European nationals, North American and Australian and New Zealand nationals, either born here, settled here with their parents or 'passing through' with corporate parental employment. We have met with children from all socioeconomic strata within these descriptions, and a variety of faith orientations. However, we have met with fewer children from other ethnic groups who live locally, such as African, African–Caribbean, south Asian or Chinese children. This list is not exhaustive, but it does reflect our concern that such children may be receiving a different quality of professional care from other children. This observation fits with patterns observed by other services that secondary and tertiary referral services are used more by majority ethnic children (Madhok et al., 1998). After all, the expression of psychosocial problems and patterns of health-care usage for children are likely to be affected by complex interactions between family and social structures and beliefs and available health-care provision. In addition, the lack of a common language, despite the use of translators, may make it much harder to communicate and express concerns about well-being, for both parents/carers and the children themselves. We might predict that these issues are more formidable for young children than for adults, because of their reliance on adults to access services for them. Children born in the UK of parents born elsewhere have experience within two cultural and language systems, which may act as a resource for communication. However, if family communication is disrupted as a result of the effects of violent behaviour, this may serve further to create barriers between the child and parents/carers, the family and service providers, and children and other concerned adults, such as teachers (Minnis et al., 2003).

In our practice we have approached these dilemmas around children and their families in a number of ways. Routinely we include discussion of cultural and religious issues in our work and in our notes. We make efforts where we can to include and involve extended family members, including older siblings, in our assessments, and sometimes in our therapeutic work. Where possible, we help family members choose their own translators, because of the repercussions within small communities of having translators who 'know' the family. Finally, we seek regular consultation from professional members of the same cultural and religious communities. We see our consultations as a means of both staying aware and thinking creatively around the various ways that different people approach some common dilemmas of living with and raising children.

As we have said earlier in the book, we do not meet with children therapeutically until we are clear that their parents/carers can prioritize their safety. However, we do meet children on their own during the course of a court assessment. This raises a host of ethical dilemmas, such as the safety of children when their mother might remain at risk, the tensions between diversity and universality in relation to child care practices, children reporting on their parents, secrets and disclosure around violent behaviour, and the consequences of possible family reunification.

Brief review of the adverse effects of domestic violence on children

In the following case we were asked by the court to do an assessment about safety in a contested contact case. The mother and the children and the father cooperated fully in the process. The context was a dispute where the mother accused the father of serious and continual physical abuse to her over the years of the marriage and the father denied all accusations against him and therefore any knowledge or responsibility. The mother and children had left the family home and stayed in a Women's Aid hostel. She and the children had been re-housed and had lived away from their father for 10 months. The family were an Asian family; in talking to the mother we needed an interpreter, but the father and children spoke fluent English. The parents' marriage had been arranged and held particular symbolic signifi-cance for the extended family because it was hoped that their union would resolve historical ongoing disputes and arguments within the family.

The parents had two older daughters who had been born in India and still lived there with their paternal grandparents. Throughout the legal process the parents both maintained implacable positions, each blaming the other. The children, a boy and girl aged 9 years and 13 years, were clear that their father had been 'cruel' to their mother but not to them.

As we had access to the reports of the social workers and the Children and Family Court Advisory and Support Service (CAFCASS) Child Reporter, we could tell that in conversation with us the two children were minimiz-ing and changing their accounts of what happened between their parents. They were consistent in begging all the professionals involved to allow them to see their father. The children told us that they wanted to see their father because they were worried about him, they loved him, he had access to money, he took them out, he made them laugh and helped them with their homework. The daughter said, 'when he is with me I forget what he does to my Mum and I think he is nice.' The son said he was bored with the whole procedure but his aggressive and distressed behaviour was the focus of anxiety for his mother and the professionals involved. What was clear was that the children were under tremendous pressure; not only was it their own dearly held wish to see their father again, but their older sisters and grandparents were also begging for a reconciliation. The extended family spoke harshly of the husband and wife depending on which family they rep-resented, but interestingly they were unanimous in their wish for reconciliation. This marriage still held such importance to the extended family in this country and in India even though many years had passed. We observed the relationship between the mother and the children deteriorat-ing as her daughter became overly mature and 'managing' and her brother became more aggressive to his mother. Even though the mother had an excellent support package she still struggled to find her voice.

The professional network consisted of eight women practitioners includ-ing the interpreter. We were multiprofessional, culturally diverse and linguistically diverse. The opportunities for misunderstanding, taking sides and blaming at either agency or individual level were considerable. Of the eight practitioners, only we and the CAFCASS Child Reporter represented the father's point of view. However, there was general agreement about the recommendations. Based on evidence of safety, we recommended that the children did see their father, first at a family centre and then in the compa-ny of an extended family member whom both parents could trust. We also recommended that the CAFCASS Child Reporter hold two 3-monthly reviews to see if safety had been achieved and what adaptations needed to be created to the safety plan. The court granted the mother an injunction which meant that the father could not come to the house. In our opinion this case represented the painful loyalty and disloyalty dilemmas in which children often find themselves.

The effects of domestic violence on children are many and various, and can be long lasting and have serious and adverse effects on a child's development. When asked, children will often say that exposure to violence in their family leads them to fear greatly for their own and others' safety, to fear a recurrence of the assault, and to report a lack of control over the violent event (Drotar et al., 2003). In addition, they will often self-report high levels of trauma symptoms. Most commentators agree that children and adolescents who live with domestic violence are at risk for post-traumatic stress disorder (McClosky and Walker, 2000), problems of coping and adjusting in everyday life and conduct problems (Davies and Flannery, 1998; Hester et al., 2000; Jouriles et al., 2001). In addition, there are a number of risk factors that may mediate a child's response to violence at home, such as early and continuous exposure to violent behaviour, and feeling helpless, victimized and overwhelmed by the emotions of rage and terror, along with the modelling of violent behaviour in family members' relationships (Drotar et al., 2003).

There may be a positive correlation between assaults on mothers by fathers, and other forms of trauma such as sexual and physical abuse (Eron et al., 1991). The British Crime Survey (1996) found that half the women who reported experiencing physical assault in the past year at the hands of their male partner were living with children aged under 16 years. Moffitt and Caspi (1998) have estimated that children living in households where fathers physically assault their mothers are four to nine times at greater risk themselves of being assaulted than if they lived in households where the adults did not behave violently towards each other. They concluded that the frequency and intensity of physical conflict between parents were linked to worse behavioural outcomes for children. Browne and Herbert (1997), in reviewing the literature on the effects of domestic violence on children, have concluded that children's development can be adversely affected by:

- learning reduced restraint and increased arousal to aggressive situations
- learning aggressive styles of conduct
- acquiring distorted views about conflict resolution in intimate relationships
- a process of desensitization to violent behaviour, which culminates in taking it for granted as part of life.

Some studies have suggested that younger children may be more at risk for the harmful effects of domestic violence, because rates of violence between intimate partners are believed to be higher in couples in their 20s. Rennison and Welchans (2000) have suggested that over 40 per cent of all households where domestic violence occurs contain children aged under 12 years. Koenen et al. (2003) reported research that suggested that domestic violence is associated with environmental suppression of IQ in young children. This finding is consistent with human correlational studies documenting the harmful effects of extreme stress on children's brain development. Thus, interventions that successfully reduce domestic assaults should also have beneficial effects on children's cognitive development. Alongside these increased risks to younger children, Hester et al. (2000) report research that estimates that two-thirds of young people in the 'looked after' system have experienced domestic violence in their lives.

The description of children as both victims and witnesses of domestic violence carries a host of possibilities for their involvement in their father's violent behaviour towards their mother or their mother's violent behaviour towards them, or other family member's violence. Children may overhear or directly observe violent assaults on their mother/carer; they may become caught up in the violence by trying to intervene and to protect her; they may be assaulted directly themselves or they may know about the violence in a number of different ways from different sources. These different levels of exposure to violence, so to speak, can have different short- and long-term effects on children's well-being, which interact with the direct and indirect effects cited above. This complexity has made it hard for researchers to gather large sample data on the mental health needs of children and adolescents within community settings. Drotar et al. (2003) reported a study with a sample of 1355 children and adolescents who had experienced a range of violent acts, most of which involved domestic violence. They implemented and evaluated a successful community-based programme, which involved cooperation between statutory agencies and targeted children's mental health needs. None of the children had previously been in receipt of mental health services. Their evaluation showed that, although the children and their families presented at a time of crisis, their living situation often reflected a chronic, multifaceted set of difficulties. Systemically speaking, it is important to gather information about the effects of violence on children's development from a variety of informants, not least the children themselves!

What contexts influence how we talk to children

For many of the children we see, domestic violence is either a 'closed secret', in that it is known within the family but with an injunction to family members that information should never be given or help sought, or an 'open secret' in that family members do talk with extended family and neighbours but would not talk, for example, to social workers or the police (Imber Black, 1993). Children may or may not feel able to talk about what they see and hear, and what they fear. Keeping domestic violence a secret is most often the result of individual and familial shame and wishing to protect the family from outside scrutiny. In the case of ethnic minority families, our experience has been that black and Asian women will often be very reluctant to call the police, believing that they will take a stereotypical view of their partners as violent and black. In these cases there are important implications for the children and for secrecy. There is very little research on children and domestic violence that reports on the additional impact of race and racism on children (Hester et al., 2000). Similarly, little attention has been paid to the effects of domestic violence within sibling groups. Children may well become isolated and their care inconsistent as their parents become traumatized, distracted and drawn into the dangers of their adult relationship. Parents themselves may have been traumatized as children and may struggle to listen to their own children now as their earlier trauma is re-evoked. In these ways we can see how continuous and repeat trauma experiences can organize family and professional system responses. However, all children are vulnerable to the consequences if domestic violence is discovered through them. In our experience, when domestic violence becomes common knowledge there is a crisis for the whole family that has different meanings for them all.

Blow (1994) has identified the following five factors that might influence therapists when they talk to children and think themselves into children's shoes, so to speak, in trying to understand the nature of their dilemmas:

1. Our theories of child development
2. Children's beliefs and knowledge about adults
3. Adults' beliefs about what is best for children
4. Children's power and influence
5. Children as learners.

We have adapted Blow's five factors for thinking about the needs of children who witness domestic violence.

Our theories of child development

Our theories of child development, moral development and attachment relationships in families and household groups will form a set of filters through which we view children and the effects of parental violence on their development. For us, betrayal is at the heart of how we understand the effects of household violence on children and young people. A fundamental betrayal of trust occurs when one parent figure harms the other parent figure and presents children with an 'unsolvable' dilemma. If fathers hurt mothers, how can boys both protect their mothers and identify positively with their fathers? How can girls identify positively with their mothers and learn that they are entitled to be safe in intimate relationships? Clearly protective factors can be present in children's lives, which ameliorate the impact of living with violence and promote psychological resilience, e.g. having a trusting relationship with another concerned adult, developing wisdom and social competence through experiences of caring for others or developing a sphere of competence in their own right, such as at sport or at school (Rutter, 1999).

However, at times, the demands on children to cope and keep up with normal routines of their daily lives might outweigh their resources to manage, both personal and interpersonal, e.g. we might use attachment theory to help us understand the negative effects on children of living in violent households, and in explaining why some children grow up to become abusive in their turn. Dutton (2003) has worked with men who repeatedly batter their women partners. In adult attachment-style terms, he would describe their attachment style as fearful/angry, characterized by a tendency to intimate dysphoria, blamed on the partner, and a tendency to ruminate on perceived hurts, culminating in explosive abuse. Looking back into the childhoods of these men, the research would suggest that a triad of early factors – witnessing fathers beat their mothers, being shamed by their fathers and being insecurely attached through unpredictable parental emotional availability – constitutes the basis of later abusive behaviour. Further, such retrospective research shows up the chronic sequelae of early trauma and highlights the need to offer men treatment to resolve their trauma symptoms. The recognition that today's perpetrator is yesterday's victim has huge implications for us as therapists working with children. The research of Whitfield and colleagues (2003) suggests strongly that children exposed to violent behaviour at home are at increased risk of interpersonal violence in their adulthood, as both victims and perpetrators. This risk is thought to be cumulative, based on the number of childhood exposures to interpersonal violence. The intergenerational transmission of patterns of violent behaviour described in the work of Dutton (2003) and Whitfield et al. (2003) lead us to pay more careful and urgent attention to the needs of children who witness violence, to assess for their safety, and to try to prevent an adverse life course pathway from developing, much as we see in the community work of Drotar et al. (2003) and in the work of Bentovim (1992) with trauma-organized family systems. The implications for preventive work are clear.

Many of these issues are found in our work with adoptive parents who are raising children who have been abused in a number of ways, including the experience of being victims and witnesses to domestic violence in their birth families. It needs to be said that sometimes the adoptive parents have full details of their adoptive child's previous life experiences and sometimes they have very scant information and discover more information in the process of getting to know their child. The following case illustrates some of these points.

> David was 4 years old when he went into the care system. He had lived with his birth parents, his two older sisters and his brother James who had learning disabilities.
>
> Life in his family of origin was chaotic and violent and his birth parents were neglectful of the needs of their children. Their abuse of alcohol and drugs overwhelmed them and they acknowledged that they could no longer care for their children.
>
> Within a year David had left his family, lived with his brother James with a foster-carer, and then was adopted, without his brother, by a couple who had no other children. David's adoptive parents, Philip and Imogen, sought a consultation with the Parents And Children Together post-adoption consultation service. They gave us a very even-handed description of an energetic little boy who had challenged them far beyond anything they had expected, but this had also helped clarify their commitment to him and to their new family. The four main areas of difficulty they wanted to discuss with us were: (1) the swings of his behaviour from passivity to extreme anger; (2) their concern about the violence in his birth family; (3) the variability within his learning abilities and his emotional development; and (4) the fact that they had to supervise all his play time with other children, for fear he might injure another child. In our experience these concerns often come to light in post-adoption work, and reflect the impact of a growing number of adoptions of older children, following government initiatives to increase the availability of adoption as a solution to some of the problems raised by needing to look after children like David.

Children's beliefs and knowledge about adults

As therapists working with children exposed to intimate violence, we are interested in their beliefs and knowledge about adults, e.g. what children think adults prefer children not to say or what they think adults cannot bear to hear, both parents and professionals! We think it is important to question actively these beliefs, in order to support parents in helping their children. In our approach to the assessment of children's safety, and in the face of marked reluctance to speak, we will always, albeit tentatively, name children's feelings and reactions when asking them what they may have seen, heard or been more directly involved in, as a way of letting them know that we will be able to listen. We speak as straightforwardly as we can about child protection legislation, what will happen to the information they give us, and what might be the consequences of disclosure, as a way of assuring their assent, if not their informed consent. What we say to children is important; it could well carry them through a difficult period.

Adults' beliefs about what is best for children

Equally we are interested in what adults' beliefs are about what is best for children, particularly during and after crises. We take the view that children know, at some level, what is happening between their parents and to each parent/carer. Developmentally speaking, children are parent watchers, in that they know their well-being is dependent partly on the well-being of their parent(s) and their parents' intimate relationship. Moffitt and Caspi (1998) estimated from their search of the relevant literature that over two-thirds of assaults in the home are witnessed by children. We meet parents who think that their children do not know what is happening, or think that they might know their parents do not always get along, and who have tried to convince themselves that this is protective for children. Given the risks of traumatization for children who witness violent behaviour from one parent to another, it is important that adults speak to children about what they know and do not know as a way of preventing harmful misunderstandings and expectations from developing.

Children's power and influence

In terms of power and influence, children are often at the bottom of the hierarchy. They seek to understand how the 'upper levels' work, in order to help their own survival. Issues of trust between parents and children are mediated through power inequalities, as is a child's need to 'parent watch', described above. As practitioners, our own experiences in childhood may well influence what we do and do not say to children, such as our position in the birth order, our gender, our faith beliefs, our sibling relationships, and so on, e.g. both of us are first-born female children, and sensitive to the kinds of tasks and responsibilities of the role of eldest, and the burdens and gratifications that flow from that role.

Children as learners

Finally, we pay attention to children as learners (Blow, 1994). We seek to understand how children emotionally process difficult, complex and painful material in relation to the people they love, and how they can develop a coherent and authentic story about themselves, appropriate for their developmental level and capabilities. Our role may be direct or indirect, supporting parents and other carers to help children attribute meaning to events, relationships and behaviours, which help them engage with the world in a compassionate manner and cope with the tasks of daily living. To that end, we work with children and with parents and carers separately and together, when safety is assured:

- to explore the effects of the abuse of power, threat and coercion in family relationships
- to explore the inability of children to consent to what they witness
- to rebuild trust in adults and establish adult responsibility where possible
- to understand the effects of fear, cynicism and shame and how secrets are created
- to create the conditions for the promotion and development of resilience.

Children's understanding of domestic violence

In our experience we meet children who are more or less clear about what domestic violence is and what the effects have been, and we meet children who minimize and deny both the actual violence and the effects on family members and family relationships. The reasons for this are many and complex, as we outlined above. It is important for us all to learn about children's views, their ways of coping with experiences of domestic violence, and what they find helpful in terms of professional responses to them and their families. McGee's (2000) research, based on in-depth interviews with children and their mothers who had direct and indirect experience of living with violence, claimed that children feared telling professionals in case they were not believed or further violence followed a disclosure.

Mullender and her colleagues (2002) make a strong plea for including children's voices in the development of child care policy and practice around domestic violence, arguing that the marginalization of children as a source of information about their own lives hampers the development of relevant professional practices. Their research with almost 1400 ethnically diverse junior and secondary school children in England challenges whether adults always make the right assumptions and decisions around children's needs in situations of domestic violence. In particular, two issues emerged from their research conversations with children and young people that had an important bearing on children's ability to cope, namely being listened to and their views taken seriously, and being actively involved in making decisions and helping to find solutions. This finding highlights, in a striking fashion, the importance of children's agency in relation to decisions taken for them and the people they love. In Mullender et al.'s study, the children seemed most impressed by those professionals who knew about domestic violence and were prepared to do something constructive in response to it.

Children's coping strategies seemed to divide into immediate adaptation and longer-term coping and adjustment. Immediate coping involved seeking safety and help, use of distraction and strategies for blocking out what is happening, supporting and being supported by brothers and sisters, and trying to protect their mothers. Mullender et al. (2002) grouped the reported longer-term coping strategies into outward-looking and inward-looking. Outward-looking coping was active and problem focused and involved talking to others, such as friends, extended family and community figures, having a safe and quiet place to go, calling the police, supporting family members and being involved in finding solutions. In our view, this is an awesome list of decision-making responsibilities which children can regularly take. Inward-looking strategies were emotion focused, and included crying, emotional withdrawal, watchfulness and hiding their emotions.

Developing a safety plan

Hester et al. (2000) provide a framework for the assessment of children's safety when domestic violence is suspected or known. They have developed training materials suitable for all professionals working with children, designed to help staff be proactive in asking whether violence is taking place at home. Their research in the UK has shown that advice, information and support offered to professionals, and from professionals to families, can be patchy and inconsistent.

When a professional worker suspects that a child may be experiencing domestic violence at home, the following questions are recommended by Hester et al. (2000):

- What happens when your dad and mum (stepdad/mum/stepmum/dad/ foster mum/foster dad) disagree?
- What does your dad or mum do when he or she gets angry?
- Did you ever hear or see your dad or mum hurting your mum or dad? What did you do?
- To whom do you talk about things that make you worried/unhappy?
- What kinds of things make you frightened/angry?
- Are you worried about your mum or dad?

When assessing a child's safety in the context of domestic violence, they recommend the following enquiries:

- What was the most recent incident of violence? Ask the child to give details of what happened: whether any weapons or objects were used, or have been used in the past; whether their mother or others were

locked in a room or prevented from leaving the house, and whether this has happened before; and whether the child knows if substance abuse was involved.
- How often do violent incidents occur? Ask the child if the police have ever come to their house and what happened.
- What does the child do when there is violence? Ask the child if he or she tries to intervene and what happens. Ask where the brothers and sisters were during the violence, and what they did.

In our experience, asking these questions of children can be experienced as both a relief at one level and extremely anxiety provoking at another. We find that using a mix of age-appropriate methods to help us ask, and to help children express themselves, can be helpful. We might use therapeutic play methods and toys to help children articulate their experiences, e.g. use of puppets helps children step back from the conversations and events enacted with the puppets. We find that most children can find ways to talk about their experiences, and their views are very helpful in planning for their safety. Lessons commonly drawn from clinical practice highlight the importance of the processes of timing and pacing around disclosure and safety planning and trust that others will believe them.

A personal safety plan can be agreed with children, which is appropriate for their age and understanding (Hester et al., 2000). The plan can include the following safety features:

- identify a safe place for children to go if there is further violence at home
- identify a person children can go to or talk to if they need help
- make sure that children know how to contact emergency services
- make sure that children understand that it is not safe for them to intervene to try to protect their mother or others, nor is it their responsibility to intervene to protect their mother.

Working therapeutically with children who have experienced domestic violence

In our therapeutic work with children who have been exposed to violent behaviour at home, we have two major challenges: (1) to help them cope with their overwhelming thoughts, feelings and anxieties, and (2) to help them and their families resume daily routines and activities, which help and support their psychosocial development. Our task is to pay attention to these concerns as best we can whether we are doing therapy or

assessment. We try to develop our relationships with the children and their household and extended family members in a way that promotes advocacy and safety, as well as using our relationships within the professional networks to develop collaboration and trust.

In our experience it is still the case that some professionals do not appreciate fully the adverse effects of domestic violence on children's behaviour and emotional responses. As we point out elsewhere in this book, we always question around the child's and other family members' safety, when we receive a referral of emotional and/or behavioural problems on behalf of children. When trying to understand children's reactivity to their contexts, and the origins and maintenance of problematic behaviour, the widespread nature of domestic violence can often feature. Once we are assured that a child is safe, we may undertake therapeutic work to help children resolve any traumatic responses, and to adapt to loss and transition. Such work presents us with a number of challenges:

- To involve the children as co-participants in the work so that their voices are heard, and their contributions are recognized, by us and others
- To help children use their imagination and playfulness constructively in the face of serious problems
- To promote positive coping while dealing with upsetting and frightening situations.

We engage children by listening and taking them seriously, while trying to get to know them apart from their problems. A golden thread that runs through our work with children involves discovering their abilities and preferences, and using these abilities as resources in solving problems. We often ask children what they would like us to know about them. We ask parents and carers what we will come to respect and like about their children as we get to know them. We ask children what they have got going for them that will help in thinking about the present difficulties.

We find out what the child has been told about coming to see us, and what they understand about this first meeting. With younger children in child care proceedings, we make sure that they know who is looking after them. With older children and adolescents we offer an opportunity to talk separately with us, and always look for appropriate opportunities to talk to younger children on their own, and with siblings. When talking to children in assessment meetings, or in therapy meetings, we find the ideas of Freeman et al. (1997) helpful in framing questions and interventions. We are keen to draw on existing community resources and social support networks that children themselves find supportive. We have adapted some of the narrative therapy practices to the particular circumstances of children who experience domestic violence, e.g. when thinking about how the child develops resilience and copes and adjusts, we help identify appropriate audiences, both real and imaginary, for the circulation of information about the child's knowledge and hard-won competence. We develop other ways of letting people know about children's dilemmas and abilities, which might involve letter writing, scrapbooks, art work, certificates, etc. Finally we take action, along with the child and concerned others, to develop and support further the child's 'communities of concern', such as children's clubs, sports clubs, extended families, school staff, project work, and so on.

The following two vignettes illustrate some of the issues that we have outlined above. The first vignette takes place within child care proceedings, when we were asked to assess the children's mother's suitability to continue to look after her daughters, one year after their father's conviction for sexually assaulting their mother.

Bobbie and June are sisters. Bobbie was 11 and June was 13 when we first met them. They come from a white British working class family. On reading the court papers we learnt that their father had seriously sexually assaulted their mother and had tried to murder her. Both girls had overhead this attack on their mother by their father. This had occurred well over a year ago. Their father had been sent to prison, and was released early, without the family having been informed. Alongside the child protection proceedings, he was seeking contact with his daughters.

We shall not discuss the wider context of this assessment, but rather want to focus here on how the girls understood and reacted to their father's attack on their mother. The court papers mentioned the father's attack on the mother, and the girls as witnesses, but none of the previous assessments had considered this as in any way significant, either in explaining the girls' subsequent 'difficult' behaviours and struggles to cope, or as part and parcel of how they managed the transitions that flowed from their father being sent to prison. As far as we could tell, no one in the child protection system had asked the girls about what they heard and saw, beyond the police witness statement.

We spoke to both girls together and separately. We asked them what they heard and saw. Their description was graphic. In particular we noted that Bobbie went into June's bedroom and got into June's bed during the attack, and then June found she needed to restrain Bobbie from going into their parents' bedroom to save their mother. June described how she had to clamp her hand over Bobbie's mouth, so that she did not call out to her mother, and further enrage their father, who she feared would turn on them. During these conversations, we learned that the girls had witnessed many physical assaults on their mother, as well as openly sexualized approaches to their mother by their father.

The girls felt some relief when their father was arrested and sent to prison. However, his early release had frightened them both. He had parked and sat in his car near their school, and thus they were the first to know.

Bobbie's fright was more evident, in that she tied up her bedroom window with string, and refused to sleep in her bedroom on her own. Both girls had stolen within the family, and Bobbie did other things that confused and frightened the adults around her, such as cutting up clothes, and making accusations of cruel and unusual punishments. We were surprised that none of the professionals involved had sought to understand the girls' responses further, and in the context of being child witnesses of their father's assaults on their mother. In fact the professional system had taken the decision to remove Bobbie from her mother's care, and seek an expert witness assessment about her mother's ability to look after her. We noted that both girls had been denied expert psychological support during the criminal court proceedings and, following their father being sent to prison, no psychological support was then forthcoming as Social Services took Bobbie into foster care. We discovered that she moved placements six times in 6 months before she was returned to her mother's care. Thus, the girls had not been helped in the aftermath of the attack, which in our view had traumatized their mother, nor had they been helped to plan around their father's release from prison because it was sooner than expected.

In talking further to both girls, we discovered that they suffered nightmares, flashbacks, heightened anxiety around reminders of the attack, including unpleasant physical sensations of anxiety, and difficulty sleeping. Although still very frightened by what had happened, and what they feared might still happen, both girls and their mother valued being able to talk through these events, to share understandings, to offer support, to process their memories emotionally, and to attribute meaning in the context of accountability and responsibility. During these conversations, Bobbie told us that she had lied about the accusations of cruel and unusual punishments. She told us that a gruff voice in her head made her do it, eventually identified as her father's voice. We were able to offer both girls further sessions, before handing on the work to a local psychologist in their community.

In this second vignette we consider the impact of domestic violence on the relational patterns within a family, in the context of a court report. We discuss the case of Ms Smith and her four sons. In this chapter we focus only on some of the psychological impact experienced by the boys and how we understood their sibling relationships. In Chapter 7, we discuss our assessment work with their mother (see p. 86).

The court instructed us to conduct an assessment and give recommendations based on our opinions about the relationship between Ms Smith and her sons, their sibling relationships, and the potential for safety and change. Ms Smith was a single-parent mother with four sons from three different fathers. We were not asked to meet with any of the fathers. In the previous year Ms Smith had suffered a psychotic breakdown as a result of drug taking and recurring depression. As a result of this crisis she had seriously neglected the care of her children and they had been taken into the care of the local authority. The boys' ages were 12, 10, 6 and 4. At the time of the assessment she was living on her own. Her sons were living with two sets of foster carers with whom she had a cooperative relationship and where she had regular contact. Ms Smith had been a victim of domestic violence during her childhood as well as in her adult relationships. She had been introduced to the use of drugs in one of her adult relationships.

We set out our assessment in the following way: (1) we met with Ms Smith four times; (2) we met the boys individually at their foster carers and twice as a sibling group (once inside at the Family Centre and once outside in the local park); (3) we observed contact between Ms Smith and each of her sons; (4) we met with the foster carers once each; and (5) we had one meeting each with the social worker and CAFCASS Child Reporter.

Although we had not been asked to meet any of the fathers it became apparent that they were not in fact invisible and visited the home regularly. The other consideration was that, although they were fathers, stepfathers and as the mother's partners potential co-carers to the children, because they were left out of the assessment they were not held responsible in any way. None of them had sought help for the family, even though they had witnessed the deterioration of Ms Smith's health and the chaotic lifestyle of the boys during her psychotic breakdown.

In talking to the boys it was clear that they had not developed sustaining or close relationships with any of the fathers, step-fathers or potential co-carers. In addition they had been physically and psychologically drawn into the abusive relationships that the men had with their mother, e.g. although Social Services had been involved and concerned about this family for some time it had been possible for the oldest boy to take the blame for a number of violent episodes on the younger children. In addition, the older boys were drawn into psychological abuse of their mother by being instructed to taunt and tease her for crying when she had been hit and were often the butt of jokes and inappropriate behaviour. They were also encouraged to fight against each other. We were concerned about the long-term effects of these experiences but also about a process of desensitization to violent behaviour and that they would come to see conflict resolution in terms of being able to use a range of bullying activities.

However, as well as a number of concerns, when we saw them together as a sibling group, we were interested in the resilience that they showed. It was clear that they maintained the ability to be concerned about their mother and her welfare. They responded to their foster carers in a range of ways but they were generally positive. The older boys now attended school regularly, although their attendance had previously been erratic because they had spent a great deal of their time looking after the younger ones. They disagreed and fell out over toys but had enough empathy for each other to 'make up' with some encouragement from their foster carers.

In our observation of contact we noticed that the boys were moving from one toy to another in the playroom sometimes cooperating with each other and sometimes not or choosing to play alone. When the social worker directed their play at one point we noticed that their play became rougher and less careful. It was our observation that when she intervened it provided a boundary against which they 'pushed'. Their cooperation became less and their competition for the attention of the adult became more. They were also capable of responding appropriately to strangers, e.g. they were appropriately cautious but warming to us and they could talk to the Court Reporter or social worker about difficult material and having a different view, but not necessarily discrediting each other. They could be tender, playful and cooperative as well as rough, boisterous and occasionally spiteful. We could see that contact could be chaotic in many ways and we probably saw more cooperation, caring and tolerance than usual because they were aware of being watched.

We also noticed that they did not develop any games or engage in creating imaginative play; nor did they talk about their foster carers. They were mostly concerned about rough-and-tumble responses and then moving on. This type of play could easily be described as age-appropriate and stereotypically 'boys' play'. In addition, they had a history of looking after each other and sometimes being the everyday carers for their mother and taking important decisions, such as when to call the police. However, in the context of their chaotic and often frightening lifestyle we thought that they would respond well to encouragement to develop their play within a more cooperative framework which could further encourage understanding of their relationships with their mother, and between themselves, and the development of their resilience. Although it was clear that they and their mother needed appropriate professional help, we were impressed by the way that they had maintained their sibling relationship and gave them credit for this achievement.

These two vignettes illustrate the interconnectedness of violence and intimidation to both children and women, e.g. the discrete categories of 'child abuse' and 'domestic violence' merge when the intention of the perpetrator is to abuse the children as a way of intimidating and controlling the mother (Hester et al., 2000). The psychological complexity for the children can be overwhelming and it is not surprising that they will be anxious and fearful about disclosing the abuse even if an opportunity did present itself.

We close this chapter by drawing out some of the practice implications for both therapists and their supervisors. We try to raise the awareness of caregivers and community practitioners to the importance of prevention and early intervention when violence in the home is known, or suspected. Similarly, we need to try to influence the legal system of decision-making, both in meetings and in texts, by using our awareness of children's needs and the systemic implications of violent relationships and the impact of living in trauma-organized systems (Bentovim, 1992). In planning and offering our services, we need to balance risk and protective factors, support parents in listening to their children, and support each other in our commitment to listen to what children have to say.

CHAPTER 6

Adults as victims and witnesses

Common knowledge, uncommon knowledge and secrets

For many of our clients, adults and children, there is a secret about domestic violence, about who is the perpetrator, who is the victim, and what this means for their immediate family, their extended family and in their community. In our work with adults, we are also listening to their experiences as children, as much as we talk to them in their adult roles and with their adult responsibilities. Systemic practice moves effortlessly from the past and the present to the future, and thus helps adults to develop a more coherent account of their own lives. Domestic violence is often a 'closed secret' in that it is known within the family, but with the injunction to all family members that information should never be given to others or help sought. However, domestic violence can also be an 'open secret' in that family members do talk with extended family and neighbours but would not talk, for example, to social workers or the police (Imber Black, 1993). Keeping domestic violence a secret is often the result of individual and familial shame and wishing to protect the family from outside scrutiny. In the case of ethnic minority families, women will often be reluctant to call the police believing that they will take a stereotypical view of their partners as both violent and black. Some African-Caribbean women have talked to us about an individually understood code that an African-Caribbean woman will not involve the police against her African-Caribbean partner.

For many parents the overwhelming secret of domestic violence is about 'keeping' the knowledge from the children. As lead therapist and in-room consultant, we believe that we have a responsibility to be transparent about our own views regarding 'child witnesses' and the intergenerational effects of trauma. We are both of the opinion that children know about the violence to their mother, e.g. whether they are in another room, out at school or playing with friends. The dependency of children requires them to learn quickly the implicit and explicit rules in their family systems regarding what is acceptable and unacceptable to be seen and to be expressed. They are consummate parent watchers and few children believe their mothers when they say they walked into the door. In clinical work we state our position with sensitivity but we will not be persuaded that we might be mistaken. The work with mothers and fathers about the children 'knowing' rather than 'not knowing' is often a painful and delicate process. Many women believe, and fervently wish, that their children are not affected and these beliefs and wishes have been a source of strength for them. We take responsibility for our own position and acknowledge and use it in our questions about:

- what our experience in this job has taught us
- other women we have met who have felt that way
- what researchers in this area have said.

This is a therapeutic, educational and three-generational stance that keeps the safety of children in mind and acts as a confirmation to the children that their knowledge and their lived experiences are to be believed.

In our experience, when domestic violence becomes common knowledge there is a crisis for the family. This has different meanings for them all. Anxiety, relief, fear, anger and defensiveness all reflect the complexity of their responses as children, parents and grandparents. Therefore, their first appointment with us at Reading Safer Families, or with any other agency, represents both a crisis and a potential turning point. Even though domestic violence may have been kept as an 'open' or 'closed' secret within the family, this may be the first time that they have been asked about the traumatizing effects of domestic violence on all family members, across the generations. This can be painstaking and slow work because the effect of taking a wider generational view has the potential to be overwhelming. However, in looking for family strengths, we expand our questions to join with the parents in the places where things are going well, or where they have tried to make a difference while acknowledging the awfulness and distress. We are not necessarily looking for solutions, but ideas that they have had and strategies that they have used with or without success. We are always aware that in these conversations parents inevitably think three generationally, as indeed we are thinking three generationally. They talk about themselves as parents to their children, but also reflect back to how it was to be children to their own parents.

As a result of domestic violence some families may well have voluntarily given up their privacy by consenting to lengthy observation and interrogation in the context of custody disputes and other child care proceedings. Other families whom we meet are mandated by the courts to attend assessment procedures. In these cases we will have read files and documents going back years into the family's history. So they will have gone from a position of guarding their family secrets, 'open' or 'closed', to a position of extreme exposure to strangers. Therefore, it is important to us to understand how they came to this point in their lives and to use this contextualization to explore the possibility of a working partnership. We discuss the effects of being blamed and shamed in the family context and in the wider context of social work agencies and the courts. We talk about this experience as being 'in the goldfish bowl' and often normalize the experience by talking about other families whose experience has been similar.

A particular dilemma of being 'in the goldfish bowl' was illustrated when the court asked us to assess a couple who had been under involuntary scrutiny by Social Services for 12 of the 14 years they had been together. They had a family of five children and the local authority concerns always centred around the parents' inability to care appropriately and safely for their children. Paradoxically, we thought that being under scrutiny for so long had led the parents to believe 'that they just about made it' every time, and the social workers to develop the idea that with intermittent interventions the care of the children was 'good enough'. Eventually with a change of social worker the children were taken into care and the father became angry and aggressive. This response from the father only reinforced the view of the local authority about the need for safety. We were asked to write a report that paid attention to the needs of the children and the family, and to make recommendations for the future. However, in listening to the family and particularly the parents, because they had been under scrutiny for so long, they had not developed an active sense of cooperation with the local authority that was authentic, nor did they appear to have developed a sense of their own competencies and skills as parents. We thought that during this process their family attitude became one of limitation, isolation and waiting for the next intervention. In our report we included an outline of our understanding of the history and the process of being under scrutiny. The court gave us feedback that they found our systemic focus, and understanding of this complicated process of scrutiny over time, very helpful in the legal decision-making process. The parents felt that we had tried to understand them and eventually agreed to cooperate with the local authority even though not all the children were returned to their care.

Developing a different sense of family time

For many psychotherapists family stories are a rich resource, but, in thinking about the effects of domestic violence on a family, it is important to expand those ideas and consider and include the particular effects of voluntary or involuntary scrutiny, intergenerational trauma and the minimization of responsibility. Many family stories do not contain a comfortable balance between 'stories about nurture and safety' and 'stories about danger' but they can and should be able to reflect people's movement through time, and acknowledge change and effort and the understanding of change in the development of 'family time'. Roberts (1994), in her work, traced the importance of family stories, and the effects of telling family stories and having them listened to with authenticity. Alongside this, she developed her ideas about the understanding of subjective and relational time and the uniqueness of the meaning of the passage of time for each family. The re-telling of family stories of competence, achievement, change and even loss is much easier than the re-telling of those stories of neglect or violence and abuse. In both assessment and therapeutic work, it is important to keep the possibilities of the future in mind, as well as developing an understanding of the 'family over time', and how this can be used positively by family members. For many families, remembering past violence or abuse is something that they do not want to do and it is hard for children to make sense of these closed doors. However, memory is constructed in the present and so these 'what-if' conversations about what is important to tell and how to tell it can open up a sense of competence and confidence in being able to help other generations understand the story and the hesitations, denial and hurt that surround it. Equally we need to be aware of our own responses and the influences that we bring to bear on the remembering, the listening and the telling (Daniel and Thompson, 1996).

For many parents the idea of telling their children about their violent behaviour and its effects, either now or in the future, or even about the work they are doing with us, seems a daunting task. However, with help and support it is possible to create the opportunity to talk in the present, and to encourage explanations and accounts of what did happen that could be given in the future, e.g. stories of apology, of reconnection and of accountability. If the account of family violence becomes a shameful secret and becomes frozen it can be unhelpful in family development (Blow and Daniel, 2002). Time is relative to the family's life cycles, and new perspectives can be gained as family members age and have distinctive experiences and develop different cognitive capacities (Roberts, 1994). We adapt Roberts' questions to suit the assessment and/or reunification work that we are doing, and to pursue our therapeutic curiosity about the 'family over time':

• In a particular account of violent behaviour, where is a person placed in relationship to the past, the present, the future?

- From what other point of view in time and perspective might it be useful to tell this story?
- If this story continues to be told within the same time frames, what are the psychological and relational implications for the family, for the couple and for individuals in the family?
- How are people positioned in their life cycle in relation to time?
- In what ways do different family members need to think about this in relation to telling and re-telling a story?

We also ask about our clients' legal understanding of their rights with regard to legal time, e.g. with regard to accessing court papers or reports in the future, or their knowledge of their children's rights or any other official enquiries that they may have made about their family history. Boscolo and Bertrando (1993) write about their understanding of time for systemic practitioners. When time is considered in relation to domestic violence, we believe that it shows in sharp relief the issues for family members of whether to trust others and the potential (or not) for change. So many of our clients believe that the past determines the present and that violence in the past is a powerful predictor of no change or unwillingness to change in the present and in the future. In addition, past disappointments will have left both perpetrator and victim with no trust in present promises and a legacy of shame and blame that they both have to challenge and to fight against from their different positions. The clarity with which we as therapists hold safety, accountability and responsibility in these conversations is crucial, but clinically it can also be a seriously anxiety-provoking position to hold. We discuss this further in Chapter 8.

Working with issues of shame and blame

In working with issues of shame and shaming, we have found the following description of shame by Mason (1993, p. 40) to be very helpful:

> Shame is an inner sense of being completely diminished or insufficient as a person; it is the self judging the self. A moment of shame may be humiliation so painful or an indignity so profound that one feels one has been robbed of her or his dignity or exposed as basically inadequate, bad, or worthy of rejection. A pervasive sense of shame is the ongoing premise that one is fundamentally bad, inadequate, defective, unworthy, or not fully valid as a human being.

In addition to this internal sense of shame most people who are violent to their intimate partners are both defended against and vulnerable to external blame. Arguably the risk of shame is higher when you want people to think well of you. Shame can be an uncomfortable signal and a threat to our sense of self. 'Healthy' shame can promote modesty, discretion and responsibility towards others, but shame can do damage. Children who are belittled by parents can feel a disappointment to their parents and grow up with a dilemma: do they risk becoming what their parents appear to want with a concomitant loss of autonomy, or do they try to maintain a different sense of self that risks losing vital support? We are most vulnerable to the effects of shaming when it occurs at the hands of the people we love, e.g. the court may pronounce a man guilty of violent behaviour and give a sentence where amends can be made, but shame, blame and self-justification are what most men describe to us!

Therapeutically we need to engage with the task of understanding why people sometimes feel better about themselves, when another is made to feel 'smaller'. We worked with a man in his early 30s. His wife had left him because of the abusive way he had treated her. He replayed his abusive actions in his mind. These memories gnawed deeply at him. Shame is often a silent emotion that requires great energy to keep at bay. He thought he could do nothing about his past actions, and did not want to behave this way in a future relationship. When we met him he had good relationships at work. However, he thought that this was fraudulent and felt that he led a double life. He was both ashamed of himself and proud that he was trying to sort out his difficulties. We talked to him about his understanding of maturity and the development of maturity, and how he could challenge the polarized views of himself, in such a way that he could knit himself back together again. Our way into this conversation occurred when we kept him waiting a few minutes in our reception area. He assumed everyone would know why he was there to see us. He felt stigmatized and was mortified. Gradually in our meetings, we helped him take responsibility for his behaviour, to practise talking about his responsibilities now, for the future and in the past, to find ways to make amends, to experiment with the thought of people knowing what he did, and talking about his regrets. He needed to get an explanation for his behaviour straight in his own mind, before he could explain himself to others and particularly his new woman friend. Gradually, through a process of confronting shame, his feelings of shame reduced as he rehearsed with us and then practised talking about his responsibilities and actions to the key people in his life and beginning the process of making amends.

Therefore, if a man is committed to resolving his problems he comes to assessment and/or therapy with well-rehearsed expectations of being blamed and probably shamed in yet another context, so our careful questions about the context of the court appearance or other professional involvement create a style that helps him develop curiosity about his intentions, how he made decisions, how decisions about him were reached and what responsibilities, either personal or familial, he may have already taken. Mason (1993) says: 'With guilt I make a mistake; with shame I am the mistake.' Developing a conversation that can begin to encompass beliefs and practices about blame, shame and guilt, both now and in the past, can then move on to thinking about responsibility and accountability and, in time, increased empathy.

For many couples, regardless of whether they are the perpetrator or victim, they both feel blamed and blaming. Blame can be described as polymorphous in that it is difficult to locate. Therefore, the question that needs to be asked is who has the power to define blame – the 'blamer', the 'blamed' or the therapist who is pulled cognitively, emotionally and morally, first one way and then the other (Furlong and Young, 1996). Conversation about the interrelational meaning and effects of being 'blamed' and being the 'blamer' can take some time, but without it there is almost no chance of therapeutic movement or change. Change is the enemy of blame. However, even though talking openly about blaming helps, it still seeps into people's lives because it is a most satisfying punctuation and a way of reaching a conclusion. We think that it is a case of accepting that, whether it is the client or the therapist, setting out blame is perversely satisfying and self-justifying. Blaming others can sometimes be a defence against our own intolerable feelings of shame. Who gets blamed, who blames and the effects of blaming are important to talk about over at least two generations. The ideal position is for us as therapists to be able to talk about blame and the effects of being blamed, without being blaming in turn. This delicate position can help to provide just enough emotional distance to introduce and discuss ideas such as 'blame habits tell more about the blamer than it does about the actions of the blamed' (Furlong and Young, 1996). Thus an interactional and intergenerational description can be introduced that helps slowly to move a couple from the immediate war zone to a more reflective position.

Case study: the effects of shame and blame between generations

The following example from our work shows the debilitating effects of gendered premises about masculinity and in particular how the intergenerational effects of family abuse can maintain deep personal secrets around shame and blame. Mr and Mrs Cane were a white British couple. Mrs Cane was referred to us from the Women's Aid hostel. She had lived there with her two children for two short periods in the last 6 months. When she threatened to leave her husband for the third time he agreed to engage in therapy. The Women's Aid outreach worker agreed to be our stable third. This was the second relationship for Mr Cane in which he had behaved violently, and this was the first-time long-term partnership for Mrs Cane. Together they had two young children and Mr Cane had three children by his first relationship. Mr Cane was violent to Mrs Cane but not in other contexts, as far as we knew.

Mr Cane described and justified his violent behaviour as a result of his being impulsive and not able to 'take the rubbish she threw at him'. Mrs Cane described her outrage at Mr Cane's assaults. She continued to blame herself for not making the relationship work but her overriding concern was increasingly about the safety of her children. When we asked her point of view about Mr Cane's position, she told us that when she got angry she taunted her husband in a way that was intended to be personally demeaning and humiliating. She believed that this was the 'rubbish' he talked about. She had also come to believe that somehow Mr Cane sought this behaviour from her. Both Mr and Mrs Cane agreed to a no-violence contract. However, in our second session Mrs Cane accused Mr Cane of hitting her and breaking the no-violence contract. He said, 'I didn't'. She said, 'you did'. He then said: 'I didn't, if I had hit you like a man you would have known it!'

Mr Cane's description of his potential for restraint shocked Mrs Cane and shocked us as the two therapists. Mr Cane said that he had to hit Mrs Cane to stop her humiliating him. Mrs Cane's response was that she would not be safe at home and she would go back into the hostel. Mr Cane agreed not to pursue or harass her and so a new no-violence contract was established in the context of their new living arrangements. In the third session Mrs Cane had stayed in the family home and Mr Cane had moved out and was living with a friend. Mr Cane had not pursued her nor had he harassed her. They had met in the street but this had not become an unsafe incident. At this point our work was focused on helping them separate safely. In our sessions they continued to discuss the implications of their separation and issues of safety. Although the sessions were tense, Mrs Cane could give her husband credit for not harassing or pursuing her and he could give her credit for arranging contact for the children at his sister's house. Our opinion was that continuing to offer them both individual sessions in this post-separation process was crucial for safety. Mrs Cane did not take up our offer because she was well supported by the outreach hostel staff. Mr Cane did agree to some individual sessions.

In our first two couple sessions, Mr Cane had made a connection between his sense of his own overwhelming impulsivity to hit out and his belief that this was triggered by his wife's taunting. It was on these issues that we focused our therapeutic time. Mr Cane told us that his father and stepfather had been violent to him as a child, and he had been taunted in a demeaning way by his older siblings. Their message to him was that he should 'take it like a man', despite the fact that he was a child. His mother had left the family when he was five. He had a few good memories of her but it seemed he had distanced himself from her decision to leave and the emotional impact that this might have had on him. He said that he thought she needed to look after herself. As a child he did not normalize his family's abusive behaviour. He knew they violated social norms but he felt deeply shamed and unworthy. He often sought isolation where he comforted himself with vengeful thoughts, and sustained himself by promising that he would be different when he became an adult. He developed an intensely individualistic view of himself and denied the potential of any relational understanding or intimate closeness. Therefore, when Mrs Cane taunted him, the trigger for his violent behaviour was not only her blaming accusations but his own memories of his abusive past and his internal shame at his own lack of integrity because of his broken promises to himself. Mr Cane had victimized himself as a consequence of his lack of self-worth. A pattern of self-blame and guilt developed which usually ended with violent outbursts on his part. Unpacking these painful issues allowed him to begin to hold an intergenerational and relational view of parental responsibility and accountability, both his own and that of his parents towards him (Jory and Anderson, 1999). It also allowed him to develop some respect for his own developmental path as a child and the efforts he made to sustain himself. For Mr Cane, defending himself against the psychological impact of these issues meant that he was constantly resorting to more and more control of others in intimate relationships, and bolstering a greater sense of entitlement to exercise such control (Goldner et al., 1990). Mr Cane came to his sessions with us for about 6 months. His separation from Mrs Cane continued without violence or harassment and a minimum of verbal abuse.

Working with women's anger and violence

Domestic violence became an important personal and political issue for feminists in the 1960s and 1970s. The Women's Aid movement in the UK, the Zero Tolerance Campaign in Scotland and the influence of the Duluth Domestic Abuse Intervention Project have raised public awareness and empowered women to speak out against domestic violence, and to seek safety for themselves and their children. The critical analysis that came out of this period has led to many important social and legal changes and infiltrated the world of therapeutic practice. It is in this context that we are able to address the problem of women's violence, and explore their motivation and the effects of their violent behaviour towards family members. Somehow, however, it seems harder to describe women's anger and aggressive behaviour than men's (Motz, 2001). Perhaps this is because a man's aggressive behaviour fits more easily into an acceptable cultural stereotype than a woman's? Or maybe because anger is not seen as a legitimate female emotion individually, culturally or according to religious teachings. Most often an angry woman client is pathologized and individual work in an adult mental health setting is seen as most appropriate. Women who live in partnerships with violent men are often angry in their own right, and angry in response to their partner's behaviour. If a woman in a violent relationship is afraid to be angry because of intimidation from her partner she cannot claim the attention of her partner or any other people to bring about change or safety for her family. It is the silencing of women in violent relationships that often makes their own anger seem unpredictable and makes it difficult for them to represent their own lived experience (Jordan et al., 1991).

Jordan et al. (1991) suggest that some women have three broad responses to their own angry feelings:

1. I am weak
2. I am unworthy
3. I have 'no right' and 'no cause' to be angry.

The third postulated response causes us most concern. If women who live in violent relationships minimize their own emotional responses and do not feel that they have the right to say 'no' to their abusive partners, does this influence their belief in their right to safety? However, women will often show anger and say 'no' on behalf of someone else, and most often it is their children. As women see themselves as being responsible for relationships, they develop important psychological strengths, but as Baker Miller points out 'these very valuable strengths have not been developed in a context of mutuality, and they have not been complemented by the full right and necessity to attend to one's own development as well' (Baker Miller, 1976; Gilligan, 1982). Therefore, leaving an abusive man who is also vulnerable and who makes the woman feel most loved and needed in the reconciliation phase following violent behaviour is a very hard task (Goldner et al., 1990). Staying in the relationship and being angry could seem like a manageable alternative, although the relationship remains dangerously static.

The woman's social and economic position and the needs of her children all conspire with this point of view. Continuing subordination of this kind can continually generate anger and depression. If the woman and her partner agree to a therapeutic intervention and the man stops his violent behaviour, this is the high moral ground anger that we so often see and hear from women. They may feel entitled to 'pay back' for the years of violent behaviour that they endured. The man, on the other hand, hopes for immediate acknowledgement and encouragement and becomes frustrated when the woman continues to be angry. She may well continue to use her strategies of humiliation, developed during the time when he was violent to her. This is a finely balanced time in therapy where the tolerance, staying power and good will of the therapists are important. If a mutuality that fosters growth in both partners is to be achieved, it is essential to have a distinction between anger and aggression. Baker Miller describes it in the following way:

> Anger seems to be an emotion we possess which inevitably prompts us to act against wrong treatment or violation of us, against injustice . . . . Anger is a vulnerable feeling. An angry person usually also feels hurt and in pain and opens this up for and to others. By contrast, aggressive behaviour is an attempt to prevail by force and to end the flow of the interaction. It is very different from real engagement with the difficult feelings that anger evokes.
>
> Jordan (1997, p. 201)

We would argue that we need to take all violent acts seriously, because of the effects on the victims, the perpetrators and the children living in their care. There is some debate in the relevant literature on the effects of women's violent behaviour on their male partners. Women's violence is often seen as self-defence, or an expression of frustration, stress and distress, and less often as an attempt to control a partner. Johnson (1995) has classified this as 'common couple violence', i.e. the non-gendered, intermittent response to life's daily frustrations and conflicts. We have found the work of James (1996) useful in this regard as she makes an important distinction for practitioners between the following: when a woman's violence occurs in self-defence or retaliation, when she lives in fear of her partner's violence and when a woman is violent towards her partner who is not dangerous and whom she does not fear. In our work, the man sometimes hears our concern about his partner's violent behaviour towards him as an affront to his masculinity, in that a 'real' man would not take a woman's violence seriously. Most often the man's response is that 'it does not hurt'! In these moments, we take care to explore what the man's right to safety might be, how the parents want to achieve mutual respect and opportunity in their relationship, what the children might be learning, and what the parents might wish they learn instead. We use future-oriented questions in this way to minimize embarrassment, but not to minimize responsibility. Sometimes we find that women use strategies of humiliation and name calling in self-defence once the violent behaviour from their partner has ceased, in much the same way as we hear women complain about this second level of psychological aggression after the violence has stopped.

We believe that women should be accountable and responsible for their own anger and aggression and should be offered services that allow the following (James, 1996):

• She should be able to go to a therapist who is not reluctant to take a moral and ethical position regarding her violent behaviour and her own concerns about her behaviour.

- A therapist who will acknowledge and understand the significant differences between women's violence and men's violence including minimization and accountability.
- A therapist who will hold her responsible for her actions.

Case example

In the following case example we try to show how we faced these dilemmas when working with a couple where both had behaved in violent and aggressive ways and how we learned this during the therapy sessions. Mr Tomas was referred to us by his GP who agreed to be our stable third via telephone conferences. Mr Tomas's mother was from a north African country and his father was white British. Mr Tomas was in his 30s. He had been in partnership with Ms Allan, who was white British and the same age. Mr Tomas had assaulted Ms Allan and she needed hospital treatment. He was distraught, apologetic and went to his GP for help. His GP called us, and we agreed to offer him six initial sessions to discuss safety issues and to see if we could be helpful to him. Mr Tomas and his partner were living apart at this time. Mr Tomas fully accepted responsibility for his actions, and did not know at this point whether his partner would take legal action against him. We discussed and agreed a no-violence contract in the event that Mr Tomas and Ms Allan should meet, because they both lived in the same neighbourhood.

> In our individual sessions with him, Mr Tomas told us that he was the second youngest of five children. His childhood had been characterized by his father's regular violence to his mother and all the children. The children were not only victims of their father's violent behaviour but also witnesses of his behaviour towards their mother. Their mother spoke English as her second language and in his early years he recalls the children helping her not only become a fluent English language speaker but also to settle into this culture. His mother kept her own culture alive for her children and Mr Tomas had a very positive sense of his inheritance from his mother. His family visited her extended family frequently. At the time we worked with him, they all planned to attend a large wedding festival of one of his cousins.
>
> Mr Tomas told us his father stopped being violent and 'became as good as gold' when his sons reached young adulthood and were as tall and strong as their father. At this age they were able to challenge their father's violence to their mother. In middle age his father became ill with a degenerative disease and when we met Mr Tomas his father was in a wheelchair and his mother was the carer. This meant that his mother was now the 'boss' and managed the family affairs in a competent and influential way. His father's illness, however, meant that he struggled with pity for his father and anger when he reflected on his childhood experiences.

In the first six individual sessions we focused on safety and responsibility. Mr Tomas said that there had never been such a violent incident between them before. He described his partnership with Ms Allan as volatile, with pushing and shoving on both their parts. We asked about other contexts in which he had been violent and tracked his development as a child and young boy. He remembered getting into trouble in junior school for fighting but remembered it mostly in the context of his father's constant reminders to look after his younger sister. He remembered his sister as a fearful little girl who often cried and found friendships difficult, so he was very protective. At secondary school he was athletic and good at contact sports and was on the school rugby and football teams. Academically he struggled to keep up but recalled that they found a place in the sixth form for him because they needed him on the teams. In this domain he was seen as a courageous player and a leader. As a young man he was often sought out if he and his friends went out drinking and looking for trouble. As he grew older he kept up his athletic activities and worked out regularly, taking pride in his strength and health. In tracking his development in this way we could ask questions such as, 'how can boys be valued for more than their physical strength?', 'if your daughter was primarily seen as a good fighter at the pub what advice would you give her?', 'looking back if you had to consult your teachers about a boy like you what advice would you give?'. Mr Tomas began to discuss these ideas with others, and was surprised when his brother-in-law told him that over the years he had begun to dislike playing squash with him because he was a poor loser. Another friend told him his wife did not want him in trouble in Mr Tomas's company, and so on. Mr Tomas began to question and review a number of issues that he had taken for granted in a rather limited 'macho' view he had of himself and his world.

After the six sessions, Mr Tomas asked if we would see them as a couple with a view to possible reconciliation. We do not like to do long-term work with men on their own, so this fitted with our expectations of hearing the partner's point of view, and establishing another no-violence contract. Thus we could address safety directly with both of them. In planning our couple's work, we offered Ms Allan two individual sessions to give her a chance to get to know us.

Ms Allan was an only child and her whole life had been affected by her parents' decision to stay together for her sake but who had constantly fought over her. Her brittleness and constant energy may well have been a result of never being able to please either parent, being constantly in a loyalty bind and being rewarded with presents by whichever parent she had pleased. This punishing cycle of psychological abuse had been a cause of unhappiness to her. We thought she needed to talk about these issues and that they were not necessarily part of the couples' work. She agreed to work with an individual therapist and so her individual sessions and the couple sessions ran in parallel.

Ms Allan talked about the effects of Mr Tomas's assault on her, in her workplace. For about 2 weeks following the incident and before her bruises cleared she found a few notes on her desk saying things like, 'it happened to me', 'I know what you are going through', 'don't go back', and so on. The effect of this was that she became a woman of some symbolic importance in the office. Conversely, Mr Tomas became an object of considerable anger and experienced personal shame within the community in which they lived and worked. We are always interested in the effects in the workplace of our clients' lives, so we asked further about the workplace attitude to domestic violence. Ms Allan told us that she was perceived to have a problem with anger management and had been sent on an anger management course as part of her annual review. She thought the course had been helpful. In hindsight, we think that we had minimized Mr Tomas's description of Ms Allan as being part of the pushing and shoving arguments. Therefore we had not followed this up by asking about her anger management. When we did ask about her anger management at home, Ms Allan told us that she had displayed her temper by throwing and breaking household objects and by driving dangerously at speed when they were both in the car.

When we met with Mr Tomas and Ms Allan it was clear that they felt passionately about each other but somehow they had not been able to decide whether or not they had a future together. Disagreements and fights ended when Ms Allan left the house to stay with her friend. In this way there was a mutual acknowledgement about a certain level of safety. However, reconciliation would mostly mean that Ms Allan would come back to the house after a few days and she and Mr Tomas would carry on as if nothing had happened. There was no discussion, verbal exchange, acknowledgement or apologies or explanations. We tried to put ourselves in Mr Tomas's shoes and asked the 'why' questions in trying to understand how these two competent and fluent people could not say what their feelings were. Perhaps Mr Tomas needed practice, or he could not commit himself or could not specifically say that he wanted her as his partner because he was not sure. Maybe he did not understand how vulnerable she felt in his presence when they argued, because he was so much stronger than her. Crucially, he did not understand that she often felt unconfident. Her employment success led him to describe her as 'a modern woman' who in his view did not need reassurance. When we looked at it from her point of view we asked ourselves, and them, 'does Ms Allan go to her other house because she is intimidated or afraid?', 'because she might lose her temper and break the relationship and regret it?', 'because she has an understanding/emotional relationship with her friend that is more rewarding?', 'because she is fearful of arguments and childhood memories?' or that maybe she could only manage the relationship in a fragmented way that gave the appearance of safety. We asked these questions using our therapeutic and reflecting process and developed a range of ideas with them as individuals and as a couple.

When we asked them about their explanations for Mr Tomas's violent behaviour on the night of the incident, they both saw alcohol as a trigger for the violence. They had the same pattern of binge drinking over weekends but not during the week. Thus they protected their employment. On the night of the assault, they had agreed to meet, but Mr Tomas met with some friends for drinks earlier in the evening, drank heavily and, because he could not drive, a friend drove him home where he went to bed. Ms Allan waited for him and had a number of drinks with her friends. When she got home she saw Mr Tomas in bed and threw a vase at him. He awoke suddenly, got out of bed and assaulted her. When we unpacked the events and decisions of that evening and their understanding, Mr Tomas continued to apologize and to maintain responsibility for his behaviour in the future. Ms Allan gave evidence of his continuing non-violent behaviour to date. However, when we asked Ms Allan about her violent behaviour and responsibility in throwing the vase at Mr Tomas, she refused to take any responsibility for her actions. Ms Allan maintained an entitlement to throw the vase because he deserved that treatment. She believed that by owning her own responsibility she was diminishing his responsibility. Her position on the high moral ground allowed her no acknowledgement of her own responsibility and she developed some resentment to us because she believed that we, in asking her to accept responsibility, were also minimizing Mr Tomas's responsibility. She chastised us for being two women and not 'taking her side'. In our sessions we consistently held Mr Tomas responsible for his actions but we could not persuade Ms Allan to acknowledge her responsibility either for her violent behaviour or for her safety. Mr Tomas and Ms Allan reconciled for a few weeks but the tensions and blame between them led to so many arguments that it was not a safe relationship. Mr Tomas decided to end their relationship, they separated and Ms Allan moved to a different area. During this time, Ms Allan continued with the support of her individual therapist. We offered Mr Tomas a few more sessions during the period of their separation.

CHAPTER 7

Therapeutic interventions and the legal process

Invisible men and their families

The last eight years have seen considerable changes in the court system and its responses to family issues. However, little seems to have changed in the public discourses around holding men accountable for their violent behaviour, whether in the courts or in the local authority. In the UK court system, all too often men will become invisible and thus may have no voice and may not always be held accountable for their behaviour. On the other hand, courts and local authorities continue not only to hold women responsible for their own safety and that of their children, but also to blame them for having any contact with the men, e.g. because the local authority is primarily a child protection agency, in cases of domestic violence, women are often strongly advised not to have contact with their partners who have been violent to them. Contact with her partner (or no contact) will be seen as evidence of the mother's ability to keep her children safe and to work cooperatively with the local authority. Mothers may be judged as competent or incompetent regarding the safety of their children in terms of whether or not the men stay away (Edleson, 1998).

In these cases, we see the local authority making a demand for certainty that does not acknowledge the lived reality and the complexity of the mother/parent/child relationship and the mother's relationship to her partner in relation to domestic violence. On the other hand, for many women, the local authority protection is crucial and provides the woman and her children with a legal frame and a foundation on which to build their own lives. It is further complicated by the fact that for many women their wish is that the violence would stop but that their relationship would continue. Their hopes can sometimes rest on the persistence of the men in contacting them and the potent wish of the children to see their father. In hindsight, many of the women whom we have met talk very convincingly about the stages that they went through before they could take the decision to be on their own, responsible for their children, financially stable and aware of and able to deal with their own loneliness, etc. A woman's personal journey towards safety and the requirements of the local authority, although they may be for the most positive reasons, do not always match up.

Jenkins (1990, p. 60), when talking about individual men and their responsibility for their violent behaviour, says:

> He is likely to want to cease his violence. However, he is also likely to be well practised at avoiding his responsibility for his action and attributing this responsibility to external events or factors over which he feels he has little influence. Attempts to address his violence will have tended to involve attempts to invite others to take responsibility on his behalf.

If men wish to avoid social workers or Court Reporters they can usually do so and sometimes there seems to be a collective sigh of relief by the professionals. We first noticed how invisible men were when we started working on court reports where fathers would simply be listed in the court papers as 'father of' and 'address unknown'. So why do fathers become invisible? We believe that there are any number of different reasons (Jenkins, 1990; Edleson, 1998; Hester et al., 2000; Blow and Daniel, 2002):

- They do not want to be blamed or held accountable.
- They believe that they can walk away without feeling the consequences of what they have done.
- They may believe that they can avoid child benefit payments.
- Their partners may agree that they will stay on the periphery of the family and will return when the court case is closed.
- They may intentionally plan to return and harass or stalk the women who opposed them.
- The male partners may continue to visit the family, invited or uninvited, without the knowledge of the local authority.
- They wish to avoid the process of scrutiny and shame.
- They fear exposure of family and personal secrets.
- They regard beating the system as important.
- They do not want alcohol or drug abuse to be revealed.
- They may be young, unwed or uncommitted fathers who are visible to the family but not to the professionals.

It is our opinion that sometimes the courts and Social Services unintentionally maintain the problem and force mothers and children into a state of deception and prolonged anxiety.

There is less psychological research about same-sex couples and domestic violence, than there is with opposite-sex couples. A paper by Potoczniak et al. (2003), which reviews existing research on same-sex

couple violence, seeks to dispel the myths that it is less frequent and not a problem. They express concern about both under-reporting and a tendency within legal and social care systems to provide inadequate protection for same-sex couples, e.g. they report cases of police and social care interventions that consider the violence to be boyfriend–boyfriend, which overlooks both the dimension of control and one of them being the victim. In their view a similar public awareness health campaign is needed for same-sex couples, in much the same way as happened for opposite-sex couples. Within this concern, we would also wish to raise the issue of men as victims of domestic violence, in terms of both physical and psychological abuse. It has been our experience that these men find it difficult to identify themselves and that there are few services for them, or ambiguous or inadequate protection, e.g. we worked with a father who had been reported to Social Services by his mother-in-law for his rough handling of his two young children. We worked with him, his wife as consultant to the work and Social Services for some months. We all thought he was making progress except his wife, who continued to express her concern that he was not changing enough. It was some months before he told us that, when he tried to intervene with his young children, say over their mealtime behaviour, his wife would punch him in front of the children and prevent him from dealing with them. When we expressed our shock at this news, he seemed shamefaced and tried to tell us that her punches did not hurt and therefore did not matter. On questioning him further, we discovered that his children punched him whenever he tried to impose a house rule. We continued the work by exploring the effects on all of them of his wife punching him, and managed to engage his wife in direct work, with Social Services support.

It has become clear to us that men are almost universally responded to within the legal system as perpetrators of violence. There are very few services for men to refer themselves legitimately. Men may have been persuaded by their partners to seek help or may be willing to take up a referral within the community. We have spoken to a number of women, over the years, who have actively sought help for their partners. Politically it has been unacceptable for a long time to put funding into services for men as perpetrators; however, we believe that women's and children's safety will be improved further only if the level of consciousness is raised regarding a range of interventions for men. The responses to domestic violence have overwhelmingly been made towards women whose male partners have been violent to them. Few service protocols have been established for working with men in this context. Interventions for men continue to be through the criminal justice system such as men's groups in association with the Probation Service or the Forensic Service. The professional view also seems to be 'in two minds'. On the one hand, services for men are viewed as essential as part of a community response but, on the other hand, the rationale for working with men is that the work is essential to help protect women and children. We would extend the moral argument, however, and assert that men are entitled to therapeutic services in their own right. Not to do so, and to tell men that we provide a service to them only to keep women and children safe, potentially compromises the development of trust within any intervention or service offered. This situation would not help men develop a sense of confidence and self-respect, the lack of which often underlies their abusive behaviour, alongside any felt entitlement to abuse those with whom they are in intimate relationships. Therapeutically, it would seem to us to inhibit understanding, compassion and human engagement (Vetere and Cooper, 2004).

Fathers' roles are complex and multidimensional in family life, and embedded in cultural and political influences. For all the above reasons we have developed some strategies to make fathers more visible. We try to challenge the notion that motherhood is mandatory, whereas fatherhood is discretionary. In court reports we gather as much information as we can and write a paragraph on each father, we contact solicitors to ask if they can extend their instructions to include fathers, we offer appointments that are flexible, and write letters and make telephone calls that are designed to encourage the men to engage with the process if they can. Men will often know that they have been ignored and for this reason they may need to be persuaded of their relevance to their children. In our therapeutic work with fathers who have behaved violently towards their partners and/or their children, we try to address a number of issues that help them take responsibility for their behaviour and to develop their ideas about change, e.g. we will always talk straight about risk of harm, to them, their family members, their family life, and their future well-being, if violence does not stop. We help them develop a sense of responsibility and pride in change by contextualizing the impact of violence in their early life. We address their attachment needs and the legacies of shame by thinking intergenerationally with them about their relationships with their father, mother, siblings, in the past and present, and into the future. We talk to men about where and how they get a sense of their own worth as men, and encourage them to reflect on cultural discourses that can both constrain and help them. We talk to men about the research associations between their well-being and their children's well-being.

We are influenced by the research on engaging men in therapy. Walters et al. (2001) reviewed the extant research and concluded that fathers are more likely to engage in family work if they have a strong relationship with their own father, see their own father more often and have an active role in parenting. When fathers are included in family work, there is no overall difference in short-term outcomes, but notably the family is less likely to leave treatment early, interparental conflict decreases, fathers are less likely to 'sabotage' the family work, and there are better long-term gains in the child's functioning. So, when working with families where violence is the issue, we are active in our approach to engaging men as fathers. We ask them directly to meet with us, rather than relying on others, or being put off by their reluctance, we offer flexible appointments to fit in with their paid work, we try to show our awareness of family diversity and cultural issues in our understanding of roles and role expectations, we recognize fathers' positive contribution to children's positive well-being, we offer meetings for the parents separately or together, and we do not ask to meet the children with the parents until we are sure that the parents have been able to prioritize safety. As two women workers ourselves, often working within female-dominated professional systems, we think that we need to be seen to be committed to including fathers in the work (Vetere, 2004).

Case example

In this vignette we consider a continuation of the case of Ms Smith and her sons, discussed in Chapter 5 (see p. 64). Here we focus specifically on our assessment of Ms Smith and the complex practical and psychological issues that she found herself dealing with and our response.

> The court instructed us to conduct an assessment and give recommendations based on our opinions about the relationship between Ms Smith and her sons, their sibling relationships, and the potential for safety and change. Ms Smith was a single mother with four sons from three different fathers who were also stepfathers and co-carers. In the previous year Ms Smith had suffered a psychotic crisis as a result of drug taking and recurring depression. As a result of this crisis she had seriously neglected the care of her children and they had been taken into the care of the local authority. The boys' ages were 12, 10, 6 and 4. The boys were living with two sets of foster carers with whom she had a cooperative relationship and where she had regular contact with them. Ms Smith had been a victim of domestic violence during her childhood as well as in her adult relationships. She had been introduced to the use of drugs in one of her adult relationships. We were not asked to meet with any of the fathers in this case and we were curious about this. The local authority said that they were not available. Ms Smith had reassured the local authority social worker that she would not have any contact with them for her safety and the safety of her sons.
>
> We set out our assessment in the following way: (1) we met with Ms Smith four times, (2) we met the boys individually at their foster carers and twice as a sibling group (once inside at the Family Centre and once outside

in the local park), (3) we observed contact between Ms Smith and each of her sons, (4) we met with the foster carers once each, and (5) we had one meeting each with the social worker and CAFCASS Reporter.

Ms Smith was living on her own at the time of the assessment. When she was living with her second partner she had an important adult relationship with his mother. This paternal grandmother was the only grandparent, or indeed the only other person, who used to visit the family. When the relationship between Ms Smith and this partner ended, the two women became estranged. However, during the assessment the grandmother contacted Social Services asking for regular contact with her grandson and with his brothers.

From the point of view of the local authority, they felt that they had made considerable efforts to help Ms Smith by social work intervention and offers of drug rehabilitation programmes in an effort to prevent her sons from going into care. The social worker thought positively about Ms Smith but felt perplexed by her lack of success. When we asked the social worker about this she thought it was mostly to do with family confusion and violence and drugs and, from her point of view, never knowing whether she was being told the truth or not. Importantly, being told the truth was about whether Ms Smith was seeing any of her ex-partners and whether she could trust her to tell the truth about her drug taking. When we asked Ms Smith about how we would know if she was telling the truth or not, she told us that seeing the social workers' words in print had been her 'biggest wake-up call'. She did not deny the accusations of neglect nor did she blame her children or professionals and she accepted her own responsibility. She insisted that she was telling the truth about her drug taking and, when she agreed to a hair strand analysis at our suggestion, the results accorded with her account. These results helped everyone to feel slightly optimistic. It was not our task to 'know the truth', but as systemic practitioners we did feel responsible for understanding the process. As part of our conversation about 'telling the truth', Ms Smith talked to us about her dilemma between the injunctions of the local authority not to see her former partners and whether she should be believed or not. She felt humiliated by the process and the conclusions that would be drawn about her honesty. While her mental health had deteriorated, her former partners had witnessed her deterioration but they had taken no action on her behalf or on behalf of her sons (also their sons and stepsons), and they had used her house as a meeting place. This left Ms Smith feeling responsible for 'telling the truth' about men over whom she had no control and who were violent and intimidatory towards her.

Although this was not a therapeutic piece of work, our assessment questions were informed by our therapeutic understanding and by feminist-informed empowerment principles (Jordan et al., 1991; Akister 1998; Seu and Heenan, 1998). When we met with Ms Smith we asked about the history of how she had reached this point in her life. She told us that as a child she had taken responsibility to get herself and her siblings into care and to achieve this had taken considerable personal risks to herself. Subsequently she had been separated from her siblings and moved between foster homes and children's homes and not surprisingly had never developed any sense of family or closeness to her siblings. She had no contact with her father and when she described her relationship with her mother she sounded anxious and ambivalent. We were curious to know how her personal experience had informed her now as a mother to her children. When she looked back she felt very strongly that it had left her with a wish that her children should know each other, to look out for each other as siblings and to have a sense of belonging – the very things she believed she had missed out on as a child. She had not developed a sense of her own self-worth in her own right or in her relationships and she had hoped that each of her pregnancies would secure a future for that particular relationship.

As we listened to Ms Smith we also took into account a number of influences, e.g.: (1) the fact that she had been involved in a number of violent relationships as a child and in adult life with men who had been her intimate partners and fathers to her children; (2) she managed a large family on benefits and her life had been marked by deep poverty; and (3) she had very few supportive emotional and social relationships (Trevithic, 1998). In these contexts we would see the task of continuing to raise a large family as extremely hard. We asked her about her beliefs about being a mother and how she understood the need for help at this time of crisis, and what the implications of this were for her. Not surprisingly, Ms Smith felt extremely ambivalent about forming a trusting relationship with any professional. She reflected on the legacies of her childhood experiences and talked about her belief that she could and should manage on her own, and how she encouraged herself to defy the odds and survive without asking for help. This defiant and inflated sense of competence and resolve helped her to cover her sense of defectiveness, irrationality and worthlessness, which is not unusual in an adult woman and mother who has been in the care system (Jordan, 1997). Her sense of individual responsibility, 'it's me against the world', provided some immediate comfort but was unrealistic and unsustainable in the circumstances. The unintended consequences were that she could not speak authoritatively with regard to her own safety nor could she speak out against her partners who acted in an intimidatory, violent and threatening way to her and her children. As a mother it made her vulnerable in that she could not allow herself to predict and ask for help nor could she act when events spiralled out of control and her children were at risk.

Her response to stress was to take drugs but this, in turn, was an even more powerful stressor. As we asked her about her relationships with her partners she began to acknowledge that what she saw as the self-administered everyday disaster of drug dependency, which spiralled into self-blame, had got too much for her to handle. She began to understand her drug taking in the context of her adult life and relational issues. Her explosive laughter at our mention of her 'right to live safely' was a poignant moment. This was not about her admitting defeat, but rather it was about her developing her maturity to know that at this point she had to do something positive for herself and her sons. In this way change, potential for change and cooperation with Social Services and the drug clinic programme began to become a possibility.

In our assessment we did not accept the invisibility of her partners and we hypothesized that they lived on the margins, visible to the family but invisible to professionals. In seeking to understand the ragged and complex issues of power and control and to introduce some legitimacy and reality about these relationships, we asked Ms Smith about her views, e.g.: (1) how she met her partners; (2) their decisions to move in together and (3) to have children, and whether they agreed to co-parent; (4) how she understood the men's violent behaviour in their relationship; (5) what effect the drug taking had on their relationships; (5) how their partnerships ended; and (6) what ideas she had about managing these relationships in the future. In this way she could talk legitimately about her partnership and attraction to her partners, as well as acknowledging the dangerous and unsafe times. We asked her in her role as mother: (1) What happened when your sons were born? (2) How did they develop a relationship with their fathers? (3) Did you influence this process? We asked her concerning the violence: (4) What effect did it have on your sons when they witnessed you being hit? (5) As a woman what do you believe is most important for you at this moment? Most importantly our questions allowed her to talk about the relational aspects of herself as opposed to her overwhelming sense of individual responsibility for her behaviour and the men's behaviour which was unintentionally being reinforced by the local authority. It also allowed us to understand her relationships with her children, her grief at being separated from them and to consider what she needed to do for them to be rehabilitated.

We have always found it helpful to consider drug taking and violent relationships as overlapping but also separate and different, e.g. in this case, the long-term effects of violence for Ms Smith started in her childhood but her drug taking developed in one of her adult relationships three years before the assessment. In our conversation, this separation of ideas about the effects of long-term domestic violence and her shorter-term drug abuse encouraged her to think about her own childhood and her present responsibility for her parenting of her children as separate. She began to differentiate between her ideas about being a victim, and those about being a survivor, relationally, emotionally and with the right to be safe. In the future it was important for her to understand the psychological needs of her sons and their complex relationships with their fathers and her partners, and her own position as their mother. We believed that as long as Ms Smith struggled to have control over her own internal psychological world, she would continue to struggle to have control in her external world of social and familial relationships. Our attempts to understand her relationships with her partners/fathers and potential co-carers encouraged her to see them as also having had responsibilities in those roles, and to acknowledge that, as her ex-partners and fathers of her children, when they saw her and her family deteriorate, they did have choices about how responsible or not they would be. Although this was an assessment and the sessions could not be developed into therapy, our theoretical position and questions did help her understand the issues of power, intimidation and control, and begin to explore her own relational ideas.

Working as expert witnesses in the family courts

Family solicitors and family court judges do not have much training in understanding family relational dynamics and child development. Family court judges are expected to make judgements about complex family cases that can have lifetime consequences for the people involved (Kreeger, 2003). Family and kin structures in our society are increasingly diverse, partly in response to changing economic and social circumstances. Arguably, the Human Rights Act will focus attention on post-adoption contact, and on sibling placement decisions and privileged sibling relationships, in recognition that they may well be a child's longest-lived relationships. Thus, it behoves us, as practitioners who work within the court system, to help solicitors and judges understand the advances in social science research by presenting our work in accessible ways.

The recent Woolf reforms recommend joint instruction and offer the clear directive that experts' responsibilities have to the court. The Children Act 1989 requires us to hold the needs of the child paramount while striving to work in partnership with parents. The Human Rights Act protects the right to a fair and public hearing in a reasonable time, and the right to respect for private and family life, which can be breached to protect the rights and freedoms of others. These two pieces of legislation have complementary aims, but hold within them, and between them, important areas of tension and relative degrees of uncertainty. Arguably the push within child care proceedings and the wider legal system is for certainty and this is where the expert witness comes in, to help the decision-making process move forward to the best possible conclusion. Since the advent of the Woolf reforms, we have increasingly been invited to 'experts' meetings'. We welcome this change in practice because it helps to identify areas of agreement and disagreement between the different perspectives. However, in the light of the Human Rights Act, our practice could take a step further, by inviting children's Court Reporters (formerly known as Guardians) and experts to take part in collaboratively devising care plans, harnessing the strengths within the different positions. If key indicators of progress are to be identified within care plans, experts can be consulted for their view. Such a process makes transparent the consideration of the balance of rights in any particular case.

The *Framework for the Assessment of Children in Need and Their Families* (Department of Health, 2000) reminds us that assessment is a process and not a single assessment event, and that it needs to be based on partnership with families and young people. Assessment should be grounded in knowledge derived from theory, research, policy and practice and, we would add, a critique of the manner by which we claim to know. Expert witness reports can become more scholarly documents and deconstruct policy and practices that may have no evidence base. However, critical social psychology and systemic psychotherapy view the notion of 'expert' as problematic. Observers are conceptualized as part of the system under observation, so that patterns and processes observed by the expert are only some of many that could be identified. There is an interaction of the observer, the method of observation and the people under observation, which gives rise to a fundamental philosophical problem. We cannot know what would have happened in the observers' absence. Experts, as observers of human behaviour, are subject to the same cultural and societal discourses as are the people under observation, introducing sources of bias into the observation that sometimes defy quantification. We could argue that bias in assessment is a cross that we have to bear and that our responsibility is to try to understand these sources of bias and reflect on how they operate in our observations and assessments. However, our concern stems from the belief that some experts may not acknowledge sources of variance in their data and conclusions, and act *as if* their knowledge is objectively knowable, rather than socially constructed, e.g. does the expert assessment take account of the impact on parenting of wider social processes such as poverty, violence, ill-health, migration and poor housing, and how these processes impact on their competence, well-being and sense of self-worth. In our experience most parenting assessments are carried out by middle-class professionals, such as ourselves, with working-class parents. We try to reflect on these class and cultural divides in our reports, pointing out where different opportunities and standards might operate in people's lives, in a class-based way (Vetere, 2002).

In our work, assessment of parenting abilities and the potential for change is carried out within a framework of at least six meetings. One or two meetings with parents, accompanied by one observation of a contact meeting, are never enough for us to explore the instructions systematically in the face of the inherent problems in the assessment process. Time to develop a working alliance with the parent(s), to assess whether they can work in cooperation with professionals and have the ability to see professionals as potentially helpful, is needed. We are not recommending that experts develop therapeutic relationships with parents, but there is no doubt in our minds that a full assessment has therapeutic potential, in that it can facilitate attitude change in the parents.

There is some debate on the use of expert witnesses in child care proceedings. They may well be over-used within the court system. However, a decision would need to be taken earlier on in the legal process that an expert opinion was not needed. Thus, those who decide would need to be trained to make such judgements, particularly with complex cases, where mental health issues are present and where a parent may have learning disabilities. In our experience, when we are asked to provide an assessment where a parent has suspected or borderline learning disabilities, we find that we are often called in too late (Green and Vetere, 2002), e.g. local services may have offered help to the family without tailoring it to the specific learning needs of the parents, and fail to understand that parents cannot generalize their learning and may well struggle to maintain their learning without regular top-up support. This example illustrates that sometimes key professional people in families' lives do not have the requisite training or experience. Under the Human Rights Act, social workers will be expected to demonstrate fairness and involvement of all relevant parties in assessments. Thus, the involvement of the expert witness brings another perspective, with all its constraints and affordances, and helps triangulate available sources of information. All of this leads, in our view, to the conclusion that experts should be required to receive consultation and/or supervision in their assessment practice – and so practice is open and accountable. It could be argued that adversarial questioning has a role to play in holding experts accountable for their opinions and their evidence base, in that it makes us think. Too often, however, in our view, it does not do that, because defensiveness becomes the primary psychological response, especially in the face of questioning from barristers trained in the criminal courts, who come into the family courts looking for work. We are not convinced that this is the best approach to decision-making and understanding. We would like to see experts supported and encouraged to critique the wider system under observation, while maintaining a reflexive stance in the face of their own biases.

CHAPTER 8

Professional issues, supervision and working in the territory

Supervision and consultation

Requests for supervision have extended our thinking, and so we have asked ourselves: 'What is different about supervision when issues of domestic violence are the highest context marker?' This question raised complex challenges and added another level to our reflections. For the most part our supervision and consultation would be easily recognizable by any systemic practitioner. However, we do believe that supervision around issues of domestic violence does differ in some important respects, and we will highlight these differences as we understand them.

Supervision or consultation requests are generally as follows:

- individuals who regularly work with issues of domestic violence and want to develop their skills and practice, in both private and public sector practice;
- a short-term piece of work regarding a specific case, perhaps by an independent practitioner;
- a team that wants to develop an agency response to domestic violence;
- an agency that requests a consultation around risk-assessment procedures;
- an agency that wants a systemic consultation about a particular case with recommendations and a report;
- a team, e.g. a mental health or disabilities team, that wants to develop their work with domestic violence but where it is seen as an ongoing part of complex case work and agency responses.

Although the variety of these requests can be seen as complex, the dilemmas for all of them concern either the process of making informed decisions about safety in the interests of the child or children, or whether therapy or other social interventions can give enough support as opposed to a social control response (Nielsen, 2002). As supervisors we carry a duty of care. We do not offer confidentiality around issues of risk, safety and harm when working with issues of family violence in any aspect of our work (see Chapter 2 for a discussion of confidentiality). Just as in our therapeutic work, we negotiate the areas of supervision that can be kept confidential, while retaining the moral and legal obligations around reporting. We would not go behind our supervisee's backs, so to speak, but we would explain why we were concerned, and discuss how best to respond.

From our point of view the first crucial task is to create a structure for collaboration with the organization requesting the supervisory task. As external supervisors, we will want to know what the supervisee's agency policies are on domestic violence, alcohol abuse and drug abuse, for example. For any external supervisor it is important to ask about the agency's model of internal supervision and what is expected of the supervisor/ supervisee task. If the organization wants the external supervisor to be the same as the internal supervisor, they will not have flexibility nor will they be able to give feedback that will allow themselves ethically appropriate responsibilities. We make a distinction in not commenting on the internal supervisor–supervisee conversation unless there is an agreement about this, but retain the ability to comment on the process, e.g. in agencies where new norms of overwork and stress are created and re-created regularly an outside supervisor does have an ethical responsibility to give feedback at a management level. Practitioners can get used to working in unsafe conditions and can become passive about seeking supervision because 'nothing makes any difference'. We would recommend that this issue of feedback should always be written into contracts or at least that a verbal agreement be made at the beginning of any piece of supervisory work. If there is no management responsiveness to feedback, these issues can get unhelpfully stuck in the supervisory process, causing considerable frustration between supervisor and supervisee. Alternatively, feedback can encourage practitioner support and agency responsiveness and the external supervisor can be welcomed as someone who has a useful 'different view'.

The following example shows the dilemmas faced by an agency that had established a domestic violence policy and wanted this to be reflected in their internal staff supervision. One of us (JC) was asked to consult around two main areas of supervisory response to their staff. First, they considered providing extra training for a supervisor who would specialize in issues of domestic violence and who would be a special supervisor on a case-by-case needs basis. Second, they considered providing training and support for the supervisors in the agency to raise the profile of this work. In the former they would have a highly qualified expert. However, the danger of this response was crisis intervention supervision, which often replicates the pattern of crisis response intervention that happens within the family. In the second proposal the raised profile around issues of domestic violence allowed a collaborative stance to be created where both supervisor and supervisee could learn together within the new framework, which helped create a new discourse around responsibility and safety.

Continued risk, responsibility and collaboration

In our supervisory work we have extended our model of risk, responsibility and collaboration and our continued commitment to putting safety first. As a supervisor, taking a legal, moral and ethical position is no different from that of a therapist. We would be prepared to advise a practitioner that therapeutic work is contraindicated, in the light of our contraindications (see Appendix, p. 104). Putting safety first in our supervisory practice in these cases offers some clarity about our role and activity as supervisors, and our relationship with agencies of social control. We monitor our activity levels as supervisors, and seek consultation ourselves around how active we think we need to be, e.g. if we are worried that the supervisee is overwhelmed by the nature of the clinical work, or the extent to which we can trust them to implement advice on safety as a priority. As in our therapeutic and court work we would be reluctant to provide supervision or consultation on a one-off meeting basis because of the importance we attach to creating a dialogue and developing an understanding of the process around issues of domestic violence.

There is an interesting dimension to this work regarding complex cases and whether or not domestic violence should be seen as the highest context marker. If domestic violence is privileged in this way we ask ourselves what effect it has on complex multi-problem cases. Of course, domestic violence is precisely what we are being asked to consider but the question is still valid, because it is the dilemma of anyone seen as a specialist. Therefore, we try to develop a collaborative process whereby we can respond to the issues of domestic violence and safety, but simultaneously develop a wider complex understanding of the case and develop a collaborative working relationship with the supervisee.

In supervision, as in therapy, our synthesis of 'live' supervision and 'live' reflecting process' enables us to develop our ideas with the supervisee(s) in the supervision session and between sessions, and to provide feedback into the subsequent supervision. It is always possible that a crisis or an event in the family will require an agency decision, e.g. children being taken into the care system, but this does not necessarily render the work invaluable to the family, or within the supervision process or the agency/

organization. Separation may be necessary to achieve safety but the relationships and the ability to talk about the impact of the crisis will stay central to the work. In our experience the most helpful way of addressing these issues is to acknowledge that none of the cases is without risk. This is the nature of the territory, which includes domestic violence.

Creating a context for supervision

In the challenging area for supervision between therapy and social control Nielsen (2002) coins the phrase 'working in the grey zone'. He says, 'Supervising this type of case puts the supervisor in an important role. The cases are a significant challenge to the supervisor's thinking, skill, and personal style'. In thinking about this 'grey zone', we asked ourselves 'what are the main responsibilities of the supervisor?' and 'what should the supervisee expect?'. We saw them as follows:

• Creating a space and a collaboration that can be trusted and where indecision, reflectivity and action will be held in equal regard.
• Clarity about accountability and responsibility: shared accountability and shared responsibility allow tension and anxiety to be contained and still encourage creative ideas.
• We believe that it is helpful for the supervisor to share with the supervisee some ideas about her style of supervision and her supervisory role. It is then possible to discuss what would be the acceptable and collaborative parameters for such a process.
• We think that it is helpful to tell supervisees that we will always ask about their personal safety. This is because it naturally needs to be part of the ebb and flow of supervisory conversation. If it is mentioned for the first time in the context of a particular case, it can have the effect of unhelpfully raising anxiety rather than acknowledging safety as a threat that runs through the work.
• We also pay attention to the emotional well-being of the supervisee and the effects that this work has on her. There may be moments when the case triggers unexpected memories that will take everyone by surprise. We will be straightforward about our willingness to be supportive within the supervisory relationship, and offer appropriate advice and referral where appropriate.
• These boundaries are also the responsibility of the supervisor when personal issues impact on her own supervisory work.
• We have a commitment to trying to maintain a balance that means we can try not to get overwhelmed or frozen by a situation nor underwhelmed and unresponsive.

Some of the supervisory dilemmas and the reflecting process

Working with issues of family violence, without adequate support and supervision raises a number of dilemmas for practitioners, such as:

- getting overloaded with information without managing to find clarity;
- practitioners getting isolated by not sharing their concerns and a resulting preoccupation with a family;
- the tension of constantly being asked to judge unpredictable behaviour;
- losing sight of competencies and resilience;
- seeking simplistic solutions;
- over-empathizing with the victim and repeating victim/rescuer positions with resulting anger and frustration over agency responses, services or management decisions.

As in therapy there is a tension to be held between seeing the case in its complexity and including domestic violence but not excluding other issues. Domestic violence is the issue that will most often promote anxiety and the need to take action. Indeed around issues of safety there may well be a bias for too-quick action, which drives the decision-making process and avoids reflection. We have found that, in a supervision session, the supervisee will sometimes want to discuss a crisis case that will include holding the added anxiety of their team. The supervisor is vulnerable to being 'swept along' by this combined need for solutions and/or action. As a result of this situation we have found a framework of questions that is often useful and reassuring to both supervisee and supervisor. The following are a number of ways in which we ask the supervisee to outline the case:

- Describe the case from the family members' point of view and then from the agency's point of view.
- What other issues or descriptions of the family do the team want us to know about?
- What does the supervisee want from supervision in terms of goals?
- What are the family doing right?
- What is the history of domestic violence in this case and what action (if any) has already been taken?
- Does the supervisee and her team (and/or agency supervisor) agree about the level of risk and/or action to be taken?
- If the family and/or agency colleagues had listened to our conversation what would they say?

Working in the territory: secondary traumatization

It is important not to conclude this book without acknowledging the impact that this type of work has on us as therapists. Systemic therapy has been slow to recognize the importance of the therapeutic relationship and even slower to acknowledge the impact on the therapist of the therapeutic endeavour. During the past eight years we have obviously learnt a great deal about developing a professional partnership in a difficult and complex area of work. We have observed, shaped and re-shaped our ideas, our responses and the development of each other's therapeutic and consultative styles. When we look to the research and therapy literature we see that very little has been written about the effects on therapists of working with everyday violence in their client's lives, compared with the literature on working with survivors of sexual abuse or with survivors of natural and human-made disasters.

Berger (2001, p. 189) writes about the nature of trauma in the relationship between the therapist and client, when she says:

> We are open to absorbing profound loss, hurt and mistrust from our clients but also to the stimulation of these human states, present in us all.

Powerful feelings can be evoked in therapists who work with trauma and the effects of trauma (Figley, 1995). In particular, we can feel overwhelmed when working with young children. Our own childhood experiences can be evoked along with our wish that children should not see certain things. Our unexamined and unacknowledged feelings can get in the way of our work, and show up as burnout, loss of a sense of professional boundaries or intensified efforts to be empathic. The risks come in the time spent listening to terrible stories, a high caseload, and little or no supervision and support.

Working with domestic violence presents any therapist with a number of personal, professional, moral, ethical and legal dilemmas, e.g. the particular tension created by working with a couple where the woman client may have been deeply traumatized by the very person with whom she wishes to be in partnership and whose behaviour she wishes to change. If the relationship is to have a future, the woman cannot be sure of her own safety until she has experienced her own safety. Therefore, the therapist(s) will also hold considerable tension about safety and responsibility for safety while the ongoing assessment of safety and safety networks progresses. This type of work can be an emotional rollercoaster which can find the therapist both working in a competent and clear thinking way and then completely unsure and over-anxious about safety. These swings of emotions, and doubts of competence, most often happen at an intuitive level and it is a very stressful experience no matter how experienced the therapist. As a result of our combination of lead therapist and in-room consultant we need to consider the impact both on ourselves as therapists and on our professional working relationship.

It is important that our reflecting process gives us an opportunity to include comments about being two white, middle-class, fluent women and also leaves us free to acknowledge our cultural values as well as our moral and ethical position. It allows us constantly to monitor our own political dilemmas and prejudices and we can comment, if we wish and if we feel it is appropriate, on the dilemmas that these issues pose to us as professionals. The feedback that we get from clients is that they find having two people in the room strange at first, but they grow to appreciate and rely on the two points of view. In terms of safety our no-confidentiality rule is helpful to us, and our clients say that they appreciate the fact that they know where they stand with us. The straight talking that we do with clients affects our relationship and we believe it encourages us to say exactly what we have to say.

In our work we believe that many of the tensions that we experience are modified by our collaborative working and our emphasis on perpetrator responsibility. In general we believe that stress in our work stems from the following:

- hearing gruelling accounts of physical cruelty;
- our disappointment when violence continues in the face of therapy or rehabilitation work;
- our risk of an inflated sense of responsibility around cases, particularly in the absence of active support from our stable third person;
- tensions around introducing systemic ideas into a conservative legal system with no tradition of acknowledging the role of emotion or passion in people's thinking and behaviour.

We respond to these demands in a number of ways. Our experience has shown us how important it is to be well informed about the effects of trauma and of wider explanatory theories. In addition we need to understand the effects of trauma on ourselves and the effects on those around us, such as client families and colleagues in the professional network, particularly when we feel anxious or angry or uncharacteristically punitive (Figley, 1995). Any working partnership needs to allow for difference as well as support. We try to be honest with each other about irrational and crazy ideas, feelings or thoughts that we might have, and we both have the right to expect a measured response from the other. In any working partnership there should be an agreement to speak out and be listened to about fatigue, irritation, over-involvement, minimization, blurring of professional boundaries, predictable responses, managing the intensity of feeling by avoiding feelings and unhelpful defensiveness (Berger, 2001).

We have developed an agreed individual responsibility that, as in therapy, the speaker and listener are equally important, e.g. if one of us is concerned about the other for some reason, we have the right to say and the other person has the responsibility to listen. There has to be an ordinary everyday way of talking about failure and impasse, as well as success.

We offer each other support for 'persistence' in the face of discouragement. It may be that some of these issues can be dealt with in our partnership/team or it may be that they are best taken to external supervision or to a specific consultation. Alternatively, we may talk to our own partners who are known within the Reading Safer Families project as the 'stable fourth'! Whatever the outcome, the responsibilities need to be shared, because working with clients, particularly with couples, can leave therapists prone to mirroring the same battles. This ongoing dialogue about the impact of what is heard, and the strategy of how to respond or how to integrate the emotions and information in a helpful way, is crucial. Sometimes our therapeutic concern will centre around a negative self-challenge, e.g. 'I should be able to hear this without feeling horrified?', or 'why do I get so upset?', which if unchallenged, could ultimately leave the therapist feeling de-skilled. New traumatic material can play on and re-open a vulnerability to traumatic material previously heard and it is often these moments that take us most by surprise (G. Smith, 2001, personal communication).

As an integral part of our work we have developed working partnerships with a number of supervisors who give us consultation and supervision to our work with families on issues as diverse as cultural and ethnic differences, gender differences, sexual orientation, legal processes and learning disabilities. We have attended national and international conferences and workshops on a regular basis, as both presenters and attendees, and we have found our conversations and experiences most influential in understanding the diversity of cultural responses to domestic violence. We seek to collaborate with community groups, and where possible engage in preventive work.

In our work we have noticed that the lead therapist's and in-room consultant's responses can become polarized and swings of emotion may be experienced, but it is unlikely that they will be the same for the lead therapist and the in-room consultant. In our experience the lead therapist usually forms a closer emotional bond with the client, but it is not always so. We seek to magnify these differences in our discussions to understand the emotional processes. These ideas lead us to analytic and psychodynamic theoretical readings about the therapeutic relationship.

We are often asked to give consultations or workshops and fortunately it is never possible to do either of these without a reciprocal learning process for us. These opportunities stretch our thinking not only about our theoretical views but also about how we support each other in our wider community of colleagues. Sharing experiences with others who understand and respond with a mix of challenge and sympathy deliberately tempers any tendency on our part to emotional complacency or defensiveness. At a recent consultation to a team about work with domestic violence, we were concerned to hear them talk about films they had seen that were helpful in thinking about domestic violence, books they had read that informed them in new ways and even a concert that had contributed an emotional intensity that one therapist thought inspirational. Although all these events are part of a good balance of everyday life and to be appreciated, it also seemed that their thinking had become so immersed in their professional concerns about their client's violent behaviour and their agency responses that they had momentarily forgotten to pay attention to the personal balance of their own pleasure management!

It is the responsibility of colleagues, supervisors and managers to pay attention to overload and the potential for 'burnout'. It is also the responsibility of supervisors to consider that some of the professional people with whom they deal will also have survived, or may be victims of, domestic violence. Many supervisors would not know whom they may be and that would be appropriate, but in this demanding area of work it is a helpful thought to carry in the rush of a busy clinical day. Every practitioner has a professional responsibility to keep up to date with the theoretical and research literature on domestic violence. This provides another helpful degree of balance and distance in relation to the intense emotional involvement of the work and provides us all with new ideas to discuss.

We also pay attention to our physical safety in a number of ways. We always work in a busy building and we do not work in the evening after the receptionist has left. We have an alarm system that is public knowledge. We do not sit in front of the door inadvertently blocking someone's exit and we do not have objects in our room that could be used as weapons. We have chosen our room to be in a neutral venue, a physiotherapy practice, which our clients tell us is helpful to them because we are more easily seen as independent. However, sometimes our colleagues need a degree of reassurance that our clients, using the shared waiting room, would not become agitated or act in a violent way; thus we see some of the emergent myths surrounding people who are known to have been violent. It is worth commenting that in eight years we have only once been concerned about a client in the waiting room.

Conclusions and agendas for the future

In this book we have set out to describe the work of Reading Safer Families and our theoretical approach to assessment, rehabilitation, prevention and therapy, and to present our work with families where domestic violence is of particular concern. We have shown how we try to differentiate responsibility for violent behaviour from explanation for that behaviour and have emphasized the importance in our methodology of our use of language, both written and spoken. Similarly we have explored issues of gender as a central analytic concept in the world of therapists and clients.

At Reading Safer Families, we have concluded, over the last eight years, that a specialist community-based project such as ours in the independent sector is appropriate, and that there is a good connection between systemic practice and the client population where domestic violence is the highest context marker. We have also learnt, through our insistence on the 'stable third', that in our community it has been possible to use systemic ideas as a way of understanding the wider legal and organizational processes and to be part of a community of professionals in a coordinated response. The feedback we receive is that it is useful for clients and has been recognized as a sophisticated and trustworthy treatment option. In the mixed economy of public and private partnerships it fits well and provides choice, and we would like to see local authorities incorporate some of our ideas. Our publications and our willingness to work with our 'stable third' mean that we have begun to be seen as supportive colleagues and in these ways we have raised the profile of domestic violence in our community.

Our shared reflection in concluding this book is that any punctuation is only part of the journey. When one of us (JC) reflects back over 29 years to 1973, when she was a member of the women's committee that started the first 'battered wives hostel' in Reading, she could not have dreamt she would be writing about these issues still. However, it is interesting to consider that today these personal and political commitments still show up in stark relief, just as they did all those years ago. Since that time the UK Women's Aid movement has flourished and become politically sophisticated and resilient. Today, for example, there are six houses in Reading offering help to single parents and ethnic minority women, as well as four open houses, so change and willingness to change have moved us forward.

It seems clear to us that at the present time there are two areas of necessary expansion in our community. The first is in response to men's violent behaviour. Politically it has been unacceptable for a long time to put funding into services for men as perpetrators. However, we believe that women and children's safety will be improved only if the level of consciousness is raised regarding a range of interventions for men. Most of the community responses to domestic violence have been made towards women whose male partners have been violent to them. There are very few provisions made for men and no service protocols established. Interventions for men continue to be through the criminal justice system. We believe that men are entitled to therapeutic services in their own right.

Most of the men we meet have been child witnesses to domestic violence, and often battered and abused themselves as children. More opportunities for men to join community-based men's groups would be a good first step, especially as they help men access other therapeutic resources as needed. We recommend that current men's group programmes be changed to include issues for men as fathers and their understanding of their responsibilities as fathers, as well as intimate partners.

The second area that needs attention is that of mothers and their children, and especially sibling groups. Traditionally, the safety needs of women and children have been responded to differently by local authorities. We meet women who leave their violent partners but have nowhere to go to discuss their worries about their children. They are often families who at many levels manage very well but often ask for specialist help from people who understand about relationships, such as family therapists. The reporting of incidents of domestic violence continues to increase. In part this is a healthy sign because more women are reporting violent incidents, and in our communities the police response has improved beyond recognition. But beyond that response there needs to be a more sophisticated understanding of the psychological effects on all family members and the impact of long-term domestic violence in relational terms.

Finally, we believe that we need to pay attention to the needs of women who are violent. Although it is true that women can be violent and their violence constitutes relational problems for their families, it is not the case that their violent behaviour always has equivalence to men's in intent, frequency, severity or outcome (Jordan et al., 1991; James, 1996). The behaviour and emotional responses of an angry woman client are often pathologized and individual work in a mental health setting is seen as an appropriate response and solution. This work requires a different political and therapeutic understanding, and women deserve to work with therapists who are not reluctant to take moral and ethical positions and to hold women responsible for their own violent behaviours.

So what about family therapists and systemic practitioners? Our experience over the last eight years is that the enduring attraction of this project lies both in the opportunity to help people find ways to live together safely and in the ever-present challenges to our systemic thinking and practice in trying to understand the complex weave of power and control in all intimate relationships. There is still much work to be done.

Contraindications for therapeutic work

The following contraindications for therapeutic work are a distillation of our practice experience and the work of those authors who have influenced us (e.g. Goldner et al., 1990; Reder and Lucey, 1995). The contraindications are an aid to clinical formulation and decision-making. They are not intended as a heuristic. Our safety methodology relies on the triangulation of different sources of information and perspectives:

1. Inability to acknowledge that violence is a problem.
2. Inability to accept responsibility for violent behaviour. We ask ourselves whether clients have the ability to listen to others, to what extent they deny their violent behaviour, whether they blame others, including professional workers, and whether there is consistency between the written reports and the verbal descriptions in our meetings. When working with a woman's violence towards a male partner, we are mindful of whether she is violent in self-defence while living with an abusive man, or whether her violence occurs apparently in the absence of physical and psychological intimidation from her male partner (James, 1996).
3. Inability to work constructively to solve problems around violence. Commitment can be explored by asking about what has worked in the past and what successes have been achieved. We want to know what resolutions have been offered and tried, if any, and in what contexts they were offered.
4. Lack of appropriate boundaries around anger expression.
5. Problem drinking and drug taking and an unwillingness to seek treatment.
6. No internal motivation for change. We would need to judge that our clients have internal motivation for change, alongside any externally induced motivation, especially as talking about anger and making a commitment to change is anxiety provoking and risky for all concerned.

7. No acknowledgement that relational factors may contribute to the problem. We search for our clients' understanding of the relationship aspects of their couple partnership and their relationships with other family members, and their responsibility towards these relationships, including their understanding of their own and others' roles.
8. Inability to empathize with the victim or to listen to another point of view. We look for evidence of empathy for the victim's experience and the developing capacity to reflect on intentions, choices and actions that include the capacity to tolerate different views of oneself in relation to others. The importance of reflective self-function (Fonagy et al., 1999) is captured in our questioning around perceived self-worth, shame and anxiety, and their effects on everyday life in the aftermath of physical violence.
9. Consistent blaming of others, either family or professional workers.
10. Lack of consistency between verbal descriptions and reports.
11. Inability to agree on the purpose or usefulness of therapeutic intervention.
12. Inability to work with professionals cooperatively, or to see them as potentially helpful. These last two contraindications are about the possibility of making a therapeutic relationship, which rests on trust, openness, listening to the views of others and the ability to accept criticism. We consider whether family members believe that a professional in a therapeutic context can be helpful. Sometimes therapeutic help is indicated, and sometimes not.
13. Extreme values, such as lack of respect for social control, and seeing women as objects rather than people.

References

Ahmad, Y. and Smith, P.K. (1989). Bully/victim problems among schoolchildren. Poster presented at conference of the Developmental Section of the BPS, Guildford.

Akister, J. (1998). Attachment theory and systemic practice: Research update. Journal of Family Therapy 20: 353–68.

Andersen, T. (1987). The reflecting team: Dialogue and meta-dialogue in clinical work. Family Process 26: 415–28.

Andersen, T. (1996). Language is not innocent. In: Kaslow, F. (ed.), The Handbook of Relational Diagnosis. New York: Wiley, pp. 119–25.

Anderson, R. (1988). The Power and the Word, Language Power and Change. London: Paladin.

Anderson, H. and Goolishian, H. (1988). Human systems as linguistic systems: Preliminary and evolving ideas about the implications for clinical theory. Family Process 27: 371–93.

Baker Miller, J. (1976) Towards a New Psychology of Women. Harmondsworth: Penguin.

Bateson, G. (1979) Mind and Nature. London: Fontana.

Bentovim, A. (1992). Trauma Organised Systems: Physical and sexual abuse in families. London: Karnac.

Berger, H. (2001). Trauma and the therapist. In: Speirs, T. (ed.), Trauma: A practitioner's guide to counselling. Hove: Brunner-Routledge, pp. 189–212.

Blow, K. (1994). Old chestnuts roasted in systemic consultancy with teachers. In: Huffington, C. and Brunning, H. (eds), Internal Consultancy in the Public Sector. London: Karnac, pp. 145–58.

Blow, K. and Daniel, G. (2002). Frozen narratives? Post divorce processes and contact disputes. Journal of Family Therapy 24: 85–103.

Blunkett, D. (2003). Home Office consultation paper – David Blunkett: Safety and Justice: The government's proposals on domestic violence, 18 June, 2003.

Bograd, M. and Mederos, F. (1999). Battering and couples therapy: Universal screening and selection of treatment modality. Journal of Marital and Family Therapy 3: 291–312.

Boscolo, L. and Bertrando, P. (1993). The Times of Time: A new perspective in systemic therapy and consultation. New York: Norton.

107

Boscolo, L., Bertrando, P., Fiocco, P.M., Meri Palvarini, R. and Pereira, J. (1994). Language and change: The use of keywords in therapy. Australian and New Zealand Journal of Family Therapy 16(2): 57–63.

British Crime Survey (1996). The 1996 British Crime Survey. Home Office Statistical Bulletin 19/96.

British Crime Survey (2000). The 2000 British Crime Survey. Home Office Statistical Bulletin 18/00.

Browne, K. and Herbert, M. (1997). Preventing Family Violence. Chichester: Wiley.

Bruner, J. (1986). Actual Minds, Possible Worlds. Boston, MA: Harvard University Press.

Burck, C. and Daniel, G. (1995). Gender and Family Therapy. London: Karnac.

Burck, C. and Speed, B. (eds) (1995). Gender, Power and Relationships. London: Routledge.

Carpenter, J. and Treacher, A. (1989). Problems and Solutions in Marital and Family Therapy. Oxford: Blackwell.

Coates, J. (1986). Women, Men and Language. London: Longman.

Coates, J. and Cameron, D. (eds) (1988). Women in their Speech Communities. London: Longman.

Cooper, J. (1989). Not just words: An exploration of how women and men use language differently and the implications for family therapy. Unpublished thesis presented for Diploma in Family Therapy, University of Cardiff.

Cooper, J. (1992). Overlapping identities. Workshop presentation, third conference on Feminism and Family Therapy, London.

Crown Prosecution Service (2001). Press Releases Archive 136/01 – Zero Tolerance for Domestic Violence. London: CPS.

Council of Europe (1986). Violence in the family. Recommendation No. R(85)4 adopted by the Committee of Ministers of the Council of Europe on 26 March 1985 and Explanatory Memorandum. Strasbourg: Council of Europe.

Crawford, M. (1995). Talking Difference: On gender and language. Sage Publications.

Daniel, G. and Thompson, P. (1996). Stepchildren's memories of love and loss: Men's and women's narratives. In: Leydesdorff, S., Passerini, L. and Thompson, P. (eds), Gender and Memory. International Yearbook of Oral History and Life Stories 4. Oxford: Oxford University Press, pp. 165–85.

Davies, H. and Flannery, D. (1998). Post-traumatic stress disorder in children and adolescents exposed to violence. Violence among children and adolescents. Pediatric Clinics of North America 45: 341–53.

Department of Health (1995). Children and Young Persons on Child Protection Registers – Year ending 31 March, 1995, England. Personal Social Services Local Authority Statistics. London: HMSO.

Department of Health (2000). Framework for Children in Need and their Families. London: The Stationery Office.

Dobash, R.E. and Dobash, R.P. (1992). Women, Violence and Social Change. London: Routledge.

Dobash, R.P., Dobash, R.E., Cavanagh, K. and Lewis, R. (1999). A research evaluation of British programmes for violent men. Journal of Social Policy 28: 205–33.

Drotar, D., Flannery, D., Day, E. et al. (2003). Identifying and responding to the mental health service needs of children who have experienced violence: A community-based approach. Clinical Child Psychology and Psychiatry 8: 187–203.

Duluth Domestic Abuse Intervention Project (1987). Year End Report to Department of Corrections, 1987. Duluth, MN: DAIP, 206 W. Fourth Street, Duluth, MN 55806, USA.

Dunford, F. (2000). The San Diego Navy Experiment: An assessment of interventions for men who assault their wives. Journal of Consulting and Clinical Psychology 68: 468–76.

Dunn, J. (1996). Brothers and sisters in middle childhood and early adolescence: continuity and change in individual differences. In: Brody, G. (ed.), Sibling Relationships: Their causes and consequences. Norwood, NJ: Ablex Publishing, pp. 31–46.

Dutton, D. (1986) The outcome of court-mandated treatment of wife assault: A quasi-experimental study. Violence and Victims 1: 163–175.

Dutton, D.G. (2003). The Abusive Personality: Violence and control in intimate relationships. New York: Guilford Press.

Edleson, J. (1998). Responsible mothers and invisible men: Child protection in the case of adult domestic violence. Journal of Interpersonal Violence 13: 294–298.

Ehrensaft, M.K. and Vivian, D. (1996). Spouses' reasons for not reporting exiting marital aggression as a marital problem. Journal of Family Psychology 10: 443–53.

Eron, L.D., Huesmann, L.R. and Zelli, A. (1991). The role of parental variables in the learning of aggression. In: Pepler, D.J. and Rubin, K.H. (eds), The development and treatment of childhood aggression. Hillsdale, NJ: Erlbaum.

Farmer, E. and Owen, M. (1995). Child Protection Practice: Private risks and public remedies. London: HMSO.

Figley, C.R. (ed.) (1995). Compassion Fatigue: Coping with secondary traumatic stress disorder in those who treat the traumatised. New York: Brunner-Mazel.

Fitzpatrick, G. (1995). Assessing treatability. In: Reder, P. and Lucey, C. (eds), Assessment of Parenting: Psychiatric and psychological contributions. London: Routledge, pp. 102–17.

Fonagy, P. and Target, M. (1997). Attachment and reflective function: Their role in self organization. Development and Psychopathology 9: 679–700.

Fonagy, P., Steele, M., Steele, H. and Higgitt, H. (1999). The theory and practice of resilience. Journal of Child Psychology and Psychiatry 35: 231–57.

Freeman, J., Epston, D. and Lobovits, D. (1997). Playful Approaches to Serious Problems: Narrative therapy with children and their families. New York: Norton.

Friedman, S. (ed.) (1995). The Reflecting Team in Action: Collaborative practice in family therapy. New York: Guilford Press.

Frude, N. (1991). Understanding Family Problems. Chichester: Wiley.

Furlong, M. and Young, J. (1996). Talking about blame. Australian and New Zealand Journal of Family Therapy 17: 191–200.

Geffner, R. and Pagelow, M.D. (1990). Victims of spouse abuse. In: Ammerman, R. and Hersen, M. (eds), Treatment of Family Violence. New York: Wiley, 113–35.

Geiselman, R. and Fisher, R. (1988). The cognitive interview: An innovative technique for questioning witnesses of crime. Journal of Police and Criminal Psychology 2: 2–5.

Gelles, R. and Cornell, C. (1990). Intimate Violence in Families. Beverley Hills, CA: Sage.

Gilligan, C. (1982). In a Different Voice. Cambridge, MA: Harvard University Press

Goldner, V. (1998). The treatment of violence and victimization in intimate relationships. Family Process 37: 263–86.

Goldner, V. (1999). Morality and multiplicity: Perspectives on the treatment of violence in intimate life. Journal of Marital and Family Therapy 25: 325–36.

Goldner, V., Penn, P., Sheinberg, M. and Walker, G. (1990). Love and violence: Gender paradoxes in volatile attachments. Family Process 29: 343–64.

Gondolf, E.W. (2002). Batterer Intervention Systems: Issues, outcomes and recommendations. Thousand Oaks, CA: Sage.

Graves, T. (1999). Duluth Wheel: Critique and revision: www.duluth-model.org.

Green, G. and Vetere, A. (2002). Parenting, learning disabilities and inequality: Can systemic thinking help? Clinical Psychology 14: 9–12.

Hardwick, P. (1994). Families and the professional network: An attempted classification of professional network actions which can hinder change. Journal of Family Therapy 13: 187–206.

Hare, R.D. (1993). The Disturbing World of the Psychopaths Among Us. New York: Pocket Books.

Hearn, J. (1994). Making sense of men and men's violence to women. Clinical Psychology Forum 64: 13–16.

Hester, M., Pearson, C. and Harwin, N. (2000). Making An Impact: Children and domestic violence. London: Jessica Kingsley.

Holmes, J. (1992). Women's talk in public contexts. Discourse and Society 3: 131–50.

Holtzworth-Munroe, A. and Stuart, G.L. (1994). Typologies of male batterers: Three subtypes and the differences among them. Psychological Bulletin 116: 476–97.

Humphries, C., Mullender, A., Lowe, P., Hague, G., Abrahams, H. and Hester, M. (2001). Domestic violence and child abuse: Developing sensitive policies and guidance. Child Abuse Review 10: 183–97.

Imber Black, E. (ed.) (1993). Secrets in Families and Family Therapy. New York: Norton.

Island, D. and Letellier, P. (1991). Men Who Beat the Men Who Love Them. Battered gay men and domestic violence. Binghamton, NY: Haworth.

Jacobson, N. and Gottman, J. (1998). When Men Batter Women. New York: Simon & Schuster.

James, K. (1996). Truth or fiction: Men as victims of domestic violence? Australia and New Zealand Journal of Family Therapy 17: 121–25.

Jenkins, A. (1990). Invitations to Responsibility: The therapeutic engagement of men who are violent and abusive. Adelaide: Dulwich Centre Publications.

Johnson, M. (1995). Patriarchal terrorism and common couple violence: Two forms of violence against women. Journal of Marriage and the Family 57: 283–94.

Jordan, J. (ed.) (1997). Women's Growth in Diversity: More writings from the Stone Centre. New York: Guilford Press.

Jordan, J., Kaplan, G., Baker Miller, J., Stiver, I. and Surrey, J. (1991). Women's Growth in Connection: Writings from the Stone Centre. New York: Guilford Press.

Jory, B. and Anderson, D. (1999). Intimate justice II: Fostering mutuality, reciprocity, and accommodation in therapy for psychological abuse. Journal of Marital and Family Therapy 25: 349–64.

Jory, B., Anderson, D., and Greer, C. (1997). Intimate justice: Confronting issues of accountability, respect, and freedom in treatment for abuse and violence. Journal of Marital and Family Therapy 23: 399–419.

Jouriles, E.N., McDonald, R., Norwood, W.P. and Ezell, E. (2001). Issues and controversies in documenting the prevalence of children's exposure to violence. In: Graham-Bermann, S.A. and Edleson, J. (eds), Domestic Violence in the Lives of Children: The future of research, intervention and social policy. Washington, DC: American Psychological Association.

Kaufman, G. (1992). The mysterious disappearance of battered women in family therapists' offices: male privilege colluding with male violence. Journal of Marital and Family Therapy 18: 233–43.

Keane, F. (1996). Letter to Daniel: Dispatches from the heart. Harmondsworth: Penguin Books.

Koenen, K.C., Moffitt, T.E., Caspi, A., Taylor, A. and Purcell, S. (2003). Domestic violence is associated with environmental suppression of IQ in young children. Development and Psychopathology 15: 297–311.

Kreeger, J. (2003). Family psychology and family law: A family court judge's perspective: Comment on the special issue. Journal of Family Psychology 17: 260–2.

Lakoff, R. (1975). Language and Women's Place. New York: Harper & Row.

Lakoff, R. (2000). The Language War. Los Angeles, CA: University of California Press.

Lamb, S. (1991). Acts without agents: An analysis of linguistic avoidance in journal articles on men who batter women. American Journal of Orthopsychiatry 61: 250–7.

Lane, D.A. (1989). Violent histories: bullying and criminality. In: Tattum, D.P. and Lane, D.A. (eds), Bullying in Schools. Stoke-on-Trent: Trentham Books, pp. 95–105.

Lie, G-Y., Schilit, R., Bush, J., Montague, M. and Reyes, L. (1991). Lesbians in currently aggressive relationships: How frequently do they report aggressive past relationships? Violence and Victims 6: 121–35.

McClosky, L.A. and Walker, M. (2000). Posttraumatic stress in children exposed to family violence and single event trauma. Journal of the American Academy of Child Psychiatry 39: 108–15.

McGee, C. (2000). Childhood Experiences of Domestic Violence. London: Jessica Kingsley.

Madhok, R., Hameed, A. and Bhopal, R. (1998). Satisfaction with health services among the Pakistani population in Middlesbrough, England. Journal of Public Health Medicine 20: 295–301.

Mason, M. (1993). Shame: Reservoir for family secrets. In: Imber Black, E. (ed.), Secrets in Families and Family Therapy. New York: Norton, p. 41.

Miedzian, M. (1995). Learning to be violent. In: Peled, E., Jaffe, P.G. and Edelson, J.L. (eds), Ending the Cycle of Violence: Community responses to children of battered women. London: Sage, pp. 10–26.

Miller, W. and Rollnick, S. (1991). Motivational Interviewing: Preparing people to change addictive behaviour. New York: Guilford Press.

Minnis, H., Kelly, E., Bradby, H., Oglethorpe, R., Raine, W. and Cockburn, D. (2003). Cultural and language mismatch: Clinical complications. Clinical Child Psychology and Psychiatry 8: 179–86.

Moffitt, T. and Caspi, A. (1998). Annotation: Implications of violence between intimate partners for child psychologists and psychiatrists. Journal of Child Psychology and Psychiatry 39: 137–44.

Motz, A. (2001). The Psychology of Female Violence: Crimes against the body. Hove: Brunner-Routledge.

Mullender, A., Hague, G., Imam, U., Kelly, L., Malos, E. and Regan, L. (2002). Children's Perspectives on Domestic Violence. London: Sage.

Nielsen, J. (2002). Working in the grey zone: The challenge for supervision in the area between therapy and social control. In: Mason, B. and Campbell, D. (eds), Perspectives on Supervision. London: Karnac, pp. 141–56.

Novaco, R. (1975). Anger Control: The development and evaluation of an experimental treatment. Lexington, MA: Heath.

Novaco, R. (1993). Clinicians ought to view anger contextually. Behaviour Change 10: 208–18.

O'Leary, J. and Jouriles, E. (1994). Psychological abuse between adult partners: prevalence and impact on partners and children. In: L'Abate, L. (ed.), Handbook of Developmental Family Psychology and Psychopathology. New York: Wiley, pp. 330–49.

Ong, W.J. (1982). Orality and Literacy: The technologizing of the word. London: Routledge.

Peled, E., Jaffe, P.G. and Edelson, J.L. (1995). Ending the Cycle of Violence: Community responses to children of battered women. London: Sage.

Pence, E. and Paymar, M. (1986). Power and Control: Tactics of men who batter. Duluth, MN: Minnesota Program Development, Inc.

Pence, E. and Paymar, M. (1993). Education Groups for Men who Batter. New York: Springer Publishing.

Penn, P. and Frankfurt, M. (1994). Creating a participant text: Writing, multiple voices, narrative multiplicity. Family Process 33: 217–31.

Potoczniak, M., Mourot, J., Crosbie-Burnett, M. and Potoczniak, D. (2003). Legal and psychological perspectives on same-sex domestic violence: A multisystemic approach. Journal of Family Psychology 17: 252–9.

Reder, P. and Lucey, C. (eds) (1995). Assessment of Parenting: Psychiatric and psychological contributions. London: Routledge.

Rennison, C.M. and Welchans, S. (2000). Intimate partner violence: Bureau of Justice Statistics Special Report. Washington DC: US Department of Justice.

Renzetti, C.M. (1992). Violent Betrayal: Partner abuse in lesbian relationships. Newbury Park, CA: Sage.

Rivett, M. (2001). Comments. Journal of Family Therapy 23: 397–404.

Roberts, J. (1994). Tales and Transformation: Stories in families and family therapy. New York: Norton.

Rutter, M. (1999). Resilience concepts and findings: implications for family therapy. Journal of Family Therapy 21: 119–44.

Saunders, D.G. (1986). When battered women use violence: husband abuse or self-defense? Violence and Victims 1: 47–60.

Serra, P. (1993). Physical violence in the couple relationship: A contribution toward the analysis of the context. Family Process 32: 21–33.

Seu, I.B. and Heenan, M.C. (eds) (1998). Feminism and Psychotherapy: Reflections on contemporary theories and practices. London: Sage.

Smith, D. and Kingston, P. (1980). Live supervision without a one-way screen. Journal of Family Therapy 2: 379–87.

Smith, G. (2001). Institute of Family Therapy conference. Therapeutic relationships workshop: Secondary traumatisation. Personal comment made during workshop presentation.

Spender, D. (1980). Man Made Language. London: Routledge & Keegan Paul.

Steinmetz, S.K. (1977). The Cycle of Violence: Assertive, aggressive and abusive family interaction. New York: Praeger.

Stith, S., McCollum, E. and Rosen, K. (1998). The effectiveness of an integrated solution-focused couples treatment programme for domestic violence, unpublished manuscript. Available from E. McCollum at Virginia Polytechnic Institute and State University, Falls Church, VA, USA.

Stith, S., Rosen, K. and McCollum, E. (2002). Domestic violence. In: Sprenkle, D. (ed.), Effectiveness Research in Marriage and Family Therapy. Alexandria, VA: American Association for Marital and Family Therapy, pp. 223–54.

Straus, M.A. (1994). Violence in the Lives of Adolescents. New York: Norton.

Straus, M.A. and Gelles, R.J. (1986). Societal change and family violence from 1975 to 1985 as revealed by two national surveys. Journal of Marriage and the Family 48: 465–79.

Straus, M.A. and Gelles, R.J. (1990). Physical Violence in American families: Risk factors and adaptations to violence in 8,145 families. New Brunswick, NJ: Transaction Publishers.

Tannen, D. (1991). You Just Don't Understand Me: Women and men in conversation. London: Virago.

Tolman, R. (1990). The impact of group process on outcome of groups for men who batter, Paper presented at the European Congress on the Advancement of Behaviour Therapy, Paris, France.

Trevithic, P. (1998). Psychotherapy and working class women. In: Seu, I.B. and Heenan, M.C. (eds), Feminism and Psychotherapy: Reflections on contemporary theories and practices. London: Sage.

Turrell, S.C. (2000). A descriptive analysis of same-sex relationship violence for a diverse sample. Journal of family Violence 15: 281–93.

Vetere, A. (1992). Working with families. In: Ussher, J. and Nicolson, P. (eds), Gender Issues in Clinical Psychology. London: Routledge, pp. 129–52.

Vetere, A. (2002). The use of expert witnesses: useful or useless? In: Rt Hon Lord Justice Thorpe and Cowton, C. (eds), Delight and Doles: The Children Act ten years on. Bristol: Jordan, pp. 107–12.

Vetere, A. (2004) Are we neglecting fathers? Clinical Child Psychology and Psychiatry 9: 323–6.

Vetere, A. and Cooper, J. (1999). Working systemically with family violence: Risk, responsibility and collaboration. Clinical Psychology Forum 127: 12–15.

Vetere, A. and Cooper, J. (2000). Working systemically with family violence. In: Singh, N., Leung, J.P. and Singh, A.N. (eds), International Perspectives on Child and Adolescent Mental Health. New York: Elsevier Science, pp. 113–35.

Vetere, A. and Cooper, J. (2001a). Losing it and owning it: Addressing responsibility for violence therapeutically. ACPP Occasional Papers No 18: Parenting – Applications in Clinical Practice, pp 39–44.

Vetere, A. and Cooper, J. (2001b). Working systemically with family violence: Risk, responsibility and collaboration. Journal of Family Therapy 23: 378–96.

Vetere, A. and Cooper, J. (2003). On setting up a domestic violence service: Some thoughts and considerations. Child and Adolescent Mental Health 8: 61–7.

Vetere, A. and Cooper, J. (2004). Commentary. Wishful thinking or Occam's Razor? A response to 'Dancing on a razor's edge: systemic group work with batterers. Journal of Family Therapy 26: 163–6.

Vetere, A. and Dallos, R. (2003). Working Systemically with Families: Formulation, intervention and evaluation. London: Karnac.

Volosinov, V. (1972). Freudianism (transl. I.R. Titunik). Bloomington, IN: Indiana University Press.

Walters, J., Tasker, F. and Bichard, S. (2001). 'Too busy'? Fathers' attendance for family appointments. Journal of Family Therapy 23: 3–20.

Wexler, D.B. (2000). Domestic Violence 2000: An integrated skills program for men. New York: Norton.

Whitfield, C.L., Anda, R.F., Dube, S.R. and Felitti, V.J. (2003). Violent childhood experiences and the risk of intimate partner violence in adults. Journal of Interpersonal Violence 18: 166–85.

Wiesel, E. (1989). Quoted in Keeney B.P. and Bobelle, M. (1989). A brief note on family violence. Australia and New Zealand of Family Therapy 10: 93–5.

Williams, J. and Watson, L. (1998). Sexual inequality, family life and family therapy. In: Street, E. and Dryden, W. (eds), Family Therapy in Britain. Milton Keynes: Open University Press, pp. 291–311.

Wilson, M. and Daly, M. (1992). Whom kills whom in spouse killings? On the exceptional sex ratio of spousal homicides in the United States. Criminology 30: 189–215.

World Health Assembly (1996). Resolution WHA 49.25.

World Health Organization (2000). Violence against Women. Fact Sheet No. 239. Geneva: WHO.

Index

10604713R00077

Printed in Great Britain
by Amazon